TRADITION
WITH A
TWIST

VARIATIONS ON YOUR
FAVORITE QUILTS

BLANCHE YOUNG &
DALENE YOUNG STONE

C&T PUBLISHING

© Copyright 1996 Blanche Young and Dalene Young Stone
Developmental Editor: Barbara Konzak Kuhn
Technical Editor: Joyce Engels Lytle
Cover Designer: Jill Berry, Artista Artworks, San Diego, CA
Book Designer: Riba Taylor, Sebastopol, CA
Illustrator: Kandy Petersen, Moraga, CA
All photography by Jack Matheison unless otherwise noted.
Front and back cover photography by Sharon Risedorph.

Library of Congress Cataloging-in-Publication
Young, Blanche.
    Tradition with a twist : variations on your favorite quilts /
Blanche Young and Dalene Young Stone.
        p.   cm.
    ISBN 1-57120-002-9 (paper trade)
    1. Patchwork—Patterns. 2. Rotary cutting. 3. Machine quilting.
    4. Patchwork quilts.   I. Stone, Dalene Young.   II. Title.
    TT835.Y683   1996
    746.46—dc20   95-38142

Published by C&T Publishing
P.O. Box 1456
Lafayette, California 94549

Printed in Hong Kong
10 9 8 7 6 5 4 3 2 1

TABLE OF CONTENTS

DEDICATION

◆

The authors wish to thank Pfaff American Sales Corp. for making wonderful sewing machines, P&B Textiles for making incredible fabrics, and the Tuesday Floozies at Bits & Pieces in St. Joseph, Missouri for all their encouragement and support. Special thanks to Dean Stone for his patience and for naming all the quilts. Loving thanks to our families for their endless love and understanding.

To Mother, in the hope that I may teach my daughters as lovingly, as patiently, and as thoroughly as I have been taught—Dalene

To my daughters, whom I have been doubly blessed to have worked with . . . Helen Young Frost, who co-authored the first books, and now my youngest daughter, Dalene Young Stone, who has proven to be an able co-author—Blanche

PREFACE

◆

Quilting is an art that dates back many generations. Young girls were taught quilting skills by their mothers, grandmothers, and aunts. Patterns and fabric scraps were passed down through the years. Quilts were made to celebrate special occasions, often a marriage or the birth of a baby. But the majority of quilts were made to keep families warm during long winter nights. Although quilts were a necessity, many quilters found the time and energy to enjoy the creativeness that came from designing, piecing, and quilting the heirloom patterns. Quilting became less of a chore and more of a labor of love.

Today, quilters share many of the traits of quilters of the past. Modern day quilters tend to their families and homes and have full-time careers, and they find the time to create the quilts that will be the heirlooms of tomorrow. Today's quilts are made to be admired, but many will be used to cover beds at some time or another. And, we are fortunate to have the sewing machines and quilting tools that enable us to create masterpieces in a minimum of time.

Within this book, we join the old and new traditions by presenting a new twist to traditional quilts with new methods and a new color flair. The older methods are still valid and work great, but the new techniques were developed to use the tools available to us today. (The cutting procedures focus on utilizing the rotary cutter and cutting mat.) We hope you will be as thrilled as we are when you finish your quilt with such ease and simplicity.

CHAPTER 1

BASIC INSTRUCTIONS

SUPPLIES

◆ *Sewing machine:* The sewing machine should be in good working condition. Keep your machine clean and oiled as directed by your owners manual.

◆ *Sewing machine needles:* Putting a new needle in your machine at the beginning of every project is a good idea. We recommend size 80/12.

◆ *Thread:* Use cotton thread or cotton-covered polyester thread in a medium shade of the project's main color.

◆ *Straight pins:* We don't do much pinning but, when you need them, they are nice to have on hand.

◆ *Scissors:* small clippers for cutting threads.

◆ *Rotary cutter with a sharp blade:* There are many different rotary cutters on the market today. We feel that the choice of which cutter to use is a matter of personal preference.

◆ *Cutting mat:* at least 20" x 24".

◆ *Rulers:* Use a small ruler approximately 4" x 14" and a large ruler approximately 6½" x 24" (at least one should have a 45° angle marked on it). You can get by with just the larger ruler, but at times the smaller one is easier to handle.

CHOOSING COLORS FOR YOUR QUILTS

When planning a quilt, selecting what colors and fabrics to use can be the most exhilarating step—yet the most exhausting. Of course, the first decision you must make is which style of quilt you want to create. You can then begin choosing colors for your quilt. The perfect fabric to start with is the one we call "just love that fabric." This fabric is your guide, both for choosing the other fabrics and the color values.

The color value of a fabric is the relative lightness or darkness of the fabric. As you gather fabrics, note that a quilt should include light and dark value fabrics with medium fabrics between the extremes. If you are unsure of the color values of your fabrics, try this simple procedure: Cut swatches from each of your quilt fabrics. Using a glue stick, paste the swatches onto a piece of paper. Photocopy the combination of swatches using a black and white photocopier. The black and white copy should show not only the value of the fabrics, but also which fabrics are darker, lighter, or of a medium value than the others in that group.

As you add to your "love" fabric, choose complementary fabrics with lighter and darker values. If the quilt is going to be blue, add fabrics with teal and purple colors, and then accent the fabrics with blue fabric that includes pink or magenta. Surprisingly, when the fabrics are combined, the quilt will still look blue. If you've decided to make a red quilt, add pink and orange colors to enhance your choice of red fabric. Many times we start planning a quilt around one fabric and find by time we've accumulated all the fabrics that the first fabric is no longer one of our choices!

No matter how many colors you have in your selection, arrange your fabrics in color value from light to dark. Blending the fabrics with a gradual gradation of value will prevent a choppy, checkerboard look. If you've included a fabric in your design that you're not sure of, take it out, and if you don't miss it, you can probably do without it. Use that "other" fabric that blends great, in spite of the little yellow flowers or the little orange triangles it may have. And try to avoid fabrics that have a light background and a dark print (or visa versa) since they can be considered both light and dark values (these prints are always hard to use).

Choosing different sizes of prints, either large, medium, or small also enhances the colors. However, you should avoid using all small prints. When all small prints are combined in a design, the fabric squares end up looking like they were sent through a food mill. However, the design of the print doesn't have to be the same; flowers, paisleys, and geometric prints work together beautifully. By placing two or three large prints together, you can produce a wonderfully lacy effect in the design.

Here is an exercise you can do if you are in doubt about your fabric choices: Cut a 1" x 12" strip of each fabric and use a glue stick to paste the strips, in the order you'll use them, onto a piece of paper. Cut across the strips at 1" intervals (the fabrics will now be 1" squares), and slide each piece down one square. This will give you a good idea of whether the fabrics blend nicely, or if one or two might not be the right choice. If your finished fabric inventory shows an abundance of blue or all pink fabrics, or if you got caught in the 1970s earth-tone color rut, try using new or different colors for an upcoming quilt. The less number of fabrics used in a quilt, the more rigorous an effort is required to get exactly what pleases you. Increasing the number of fabrics, normally from eight to ten, makes it easier to attain a pleasing look. Choosing which fabrics to use for any style of quilt is based on several other factors: color theory components of monochromatic, analogous, complementary, and primary colors, in addition to the separate applications of tints, shades, and tones, *etc*. These color components are part of the many guidelines to help you choose which fabrics are best. However, no matter how closely you study the guidelines and suggestions, the colors you use should be based ultimately on your personal decision of what colors look good to you. The range of fabric and color choices available today is never

ending. Be daring and adventurous. Try colors and shades that you'd never dreamed of using before. (We can't think of anything more exciting than pulling the fabrics for a new quilt.) But, whatever your efforts are on any of the quilts in this book, we hope that you have as much fun as we have had.

EXPLANATION OF FABRIC WIDTHS

The width of fabrics vary. Most bolts of fabric are sold as 44"/45" widths; yet, there are times when these fabrics are not quite as wide. To accommodate for the discrepancy, we have figured yardage requirements and strip yields throughout this book based on a 42" width. We do not recommend trimming the selvages off before cutting strips or sewing the strip sets together because the selvages will be cut off when you square up the strip sets before cutting the sections.

CUTTING ACCURATE STRIPS

All of the quilts constructed in this book start with strips. Cutting accurate and straight strips is a very critical step when creating these quilts—critical, but not difficult. To begin cutting strips, start with a length of fabric with which you are comfortable. A good rule of thumb is to work with a length of fabric that fits your cutting mat. For example, if you need to cut four 2½" strips, first cut a piece of fabric about 11" by the width of the fabric. Or, 4 x 2½" = 10" plus an additional 1" for squaring up the fabric. If you need to cut twenty 2½" strips, you may want to cut two lengths of fabric about 26" rather than one length of 52". This gives 20 x 2½" = 50" plus about 2" for a total of 52". Divide the strip by 2 = 26", since the two smaller pieces are much easier to handle.

You must press the fabric to remove any wrinkles or creases before cutting the strips. Then, fold the fabric in half, selvage to selvage, and lay it on your cutting mat. Align the selvages with each other. (It is unlikely that the cut edges of the fabric will be even.) Keep the fabric flat without ruffles or waves along the fold. If the fabric does ruffle, try sliding the top layer to one side while keeping the selvages even, then once the fabric is flat, fold the fabric again into fourths, bringing the folded edge even with the selvages. You are now ready to square up your fabric.

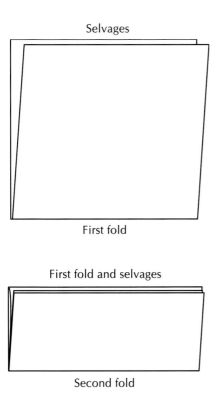

Selvages

First fold

First fold and selvages

Second fold

Line up the folded edge of the fabric that's closest to you along a permanent inch mark on your cutting mat. Lay your ruler at a right angle to the inch mark at the right end of your fabric, and align the long edge of your ruler with a vertical inch line on your mat. Holding your ruler with your left hand, cut a straight line using the rotary cutter in your right hand. (Hold your rotary cutter so the handle is tilted slightly away from your ruler and the blade points toward the ruler at a very slight angle.) If you are left-handed, simply reverse the left and right directions above. Your fabric should now have a squared end.

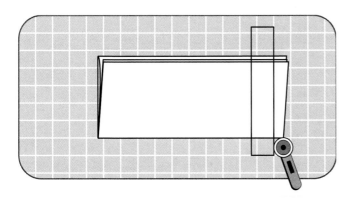

Carefully turn your cutting mat, with the fabric still on it, so the straight edge is now to your left. Lay your ruler on the left end of the fabric and measure the width of the strip needed through the ruler. Hold the ruler with your left hand and cut with your right hand. Notice that the strip you will cut will be under your ruler.

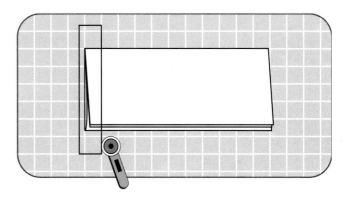

To check that you are cutting straight strips, open the first strip and lay it on a table. It should have straight cut edges without any slight angle.

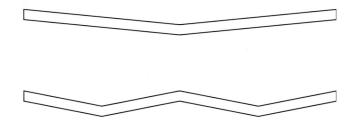

If you have a 'V' or a 'W' cut strip, repeat the folding and cutting procedures. After you have cut a straight strip, cut the remainder of the strips needed. As you cut, check that your fabric isn't slipping on the mat and that the folded edges stay aligned with the horizontal line on your mat. Also, as you cut the strips, try to keep the ruler at a right angle to the folded edge of the fabric. Align the ruler with the edge of the fabric as well as the vertical lines on the cutting mat. After cutting a number of strips, you may have to square up your fabric again.

All of the strips are cut selvage to selvage. A half strip (or half strip set) is a full strip cut in half that ends up measuring at least 21" long. A quarter strip is a full strip cut in fourths that ends up measuring at least 10½" long.

SEAM ALLOWANCES

All of the patterns in this book call for a "scant" ¼" seam allowance. This is because a "full" ¼" seam allowance leaves the squares a bit smaller than the full finished size. You can think of a scant ¼" seam allowance as ¼" less one thread width. To check your scant seam allowance, we recommend the following test: Cut three strips of fabrics to measure 1½" x 6". Sew the strips together along the long edges, and press the seam allowances away from the center strip. Now, measure across the three strips. This measurement should be 3½" from raw edge to raw edge. If your strip set measures more than 3½", try again using larger seams. If your strip set measures less than 3½", try again using smaller seams.

The width of the seam allowance you use when sewing can make all the difference in the final result of your piecing. Almost all quiltmakers use a ¼" seam allowance. While this is a very important point, a consistent seam allowance is just as important. We stress the importance of a consistent seam allowance as well as a scant ¼" seam allowance. You may find that adding a seam guide on your machine will be very helpful—as long as the guide is secure and can not be moved easily.

SEWING THE STRIP SETS

All of the quilts constructed in this book require strip sets. Strip sets are merely groups of strips sewn together in a predetermined order. When sewing the strip sets, always start with the top strip of each set. Keep track of this top strip as you sew the sets, and cut the sections, by using a sticky note (as explained in the Helpful Hints section on page 16). To sew the strip sets together, place the first strip face up on your machine, and then place the second strip face down on the first, matching the selvages. Sew the strips together with a scant ¼" seam allowance. As you sew the strips, don't hold the strips taut or the fabric could stretch. Nor do you want to push the strips through your machine, or the fabric could ruffle. Let your machine feed the fabric through. (It is unlikely that the selvages at the end of the strips will come out even, so don't let this worry you— they will be trimmed off later.)

To chain piece the strips sets, do not cut your threads after sewing the first two strips together. Sew past the strip ends and then place the first and

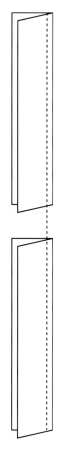

second strips of the next strip set under your machine's foot. (You may have to lift your pressure foot to ease the strips under the foot until the feed dog catches the fabric.)

Leave the threads intact between the strip sets, after joining all of the first and second strips. Start back at the first strip set. Open the two strips and place the third strip face down on the second strip. Stitch together, matching the edges. Add all of the third strips in each set. Continue working in this manner, adding all of the needed strips in each strip set. After the strip sets are sewn, cut the threads between the sets.

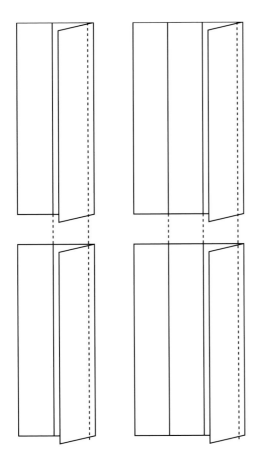

PRESSING THE STRIP SETS

Press the seam allowances in the directions shown in the individual quilt instructions. Later, as you sew the cut sections together, the seam allowances will nest together in alternate directions at each corner. As you press the seams, try not to stretch the strips or your strip sets could distort. We recommend pressing first from the wrong side of the strips, and then turning the strips over and pressing on the right side to iron out any pleats you may have along the seam lines.

STACKING AND CUTTING STRIP SETS INTO SECTIONS

Now that the strip sets are sewn and pressed, they need to be cut into sections at the width specified in the individual instructions for each quilt. You can cut one strip set at a time by aligning the strip on your cutting mat, using a horizontal inch line, and then squaring off the end as you did when cutting the strips. (Then you simply cut each section at the increment required.) But, it is much more time efficient to stack and cut several strip sets at once.

To stack the strip sets, lay the first strip face down on the mat, aligning the long edge along a horizontal inch line on your mat. Lay the second strip face down upon the first, staggering the second strip approximately ⅜" higher than the first. This will distribute the seam allowances for ease in cutting multiple strips. Stack as many strips as you are comfortable with and that can be cut accurately at one time. Then square up the right end of the strip sets in the same manner as you squared up the fabric when cutting the strips.

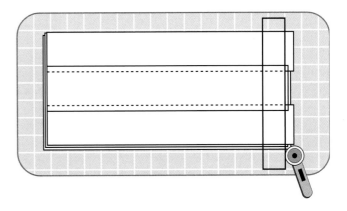

Turn the mat around so the squared end is to your left, and cut the sections at the width indicated in the individual quilt instructions. It might be necessary to square up your strips again after cutting a number of sections. It is helpful to keep one or two of the inch markings on your ruler aligned with one or two of the seam lines in the strip set.

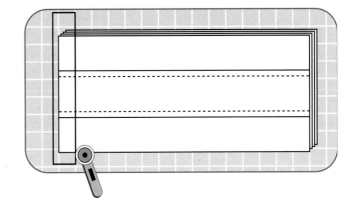

STACKING THE CUT SECTIONS AND SEWING THE UNITS

The cut sections are sewn together to make units or blocks. Blocks usually require three, five, or seven sections to complete, while a unit requires many more (considering a unit usually spans the width of the quilt). If using an even number of fabrics in a quilt, the seams in the sections will be pressed in alternating directions (the first to the right, then the second to the left, and the third to the right, *etc.*). The adjoining section will then have the seams pressed in the opposing direction (the first to the left, the second to the right, the third to the left). This allows the seam allowances of the two sections to nest together and distribute the thickness of the seams. It also aids in matching the seam lines accurately. When using an uneven number of fabrics in a quilt, the sections will have all the seam allowances pressed in one direction and the seams of the adjoining section pressed in the opposite direction. This also results in the seams nesting together.

Stack the sections in the order they will be sewn into units. When stitching the cut sections together, line up the top edge of each section and check that the seams are aligned with one another. Following the chart in each quilt project, stack one section at a time for each main unit and then sew each unit in the same manner. Notice that in some of the quilts that the unit, if folded in half, is a mirror image from the center section that divides the two halves. So, if you stack the sections from left to right, you can sew them together from right to left without any problem. Stitch with a scant ¼" seam allowance.

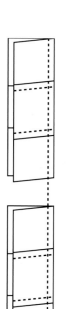

To chain piece the units, stitch past the bottom of the sections and place the first two sections of the next unit on the machine and begin sewing. Note that some of the designs require various sections to be turned upside down or reversed. As you stack these sections, be sure to reverse their direction.

Once the first two sections of the required units are joined, start back at the first unit and add the third section to all of the units, then the fourth, and *sew on*. Press these seams as directed in the individual quilt instructions.

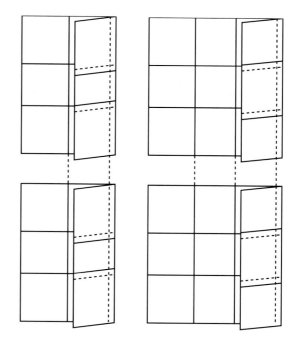

ADDING BORDERS TO YOUR QUILT TOP

Whether a border is a simple strip of fabric, an elaborate patchwork design, or something simple with an accent or two, borders are the ideal way to finish or "frame" your quilt top. Besides having an aesthetic quality, a border can be used for the very practical purpose of making a quilt larger.

We have not included border yardage requirements with most of the quilts in this book, as we did not want to limit each quilt to one size. Instead, we have provided you with simple instructions to figure the yardage for the border width of your choice. You can also decide between a right angle border and a mitered-corner border. Mitered borders are appropriate when using a border print or striped fabric for your borders, since the design of the fabric will be continuous around the quilt.

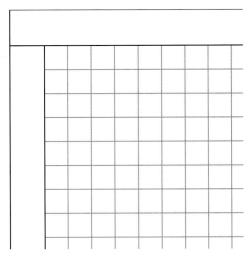

Right angle border

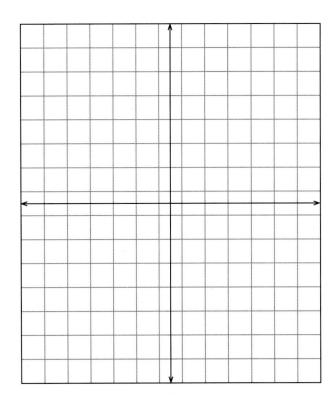

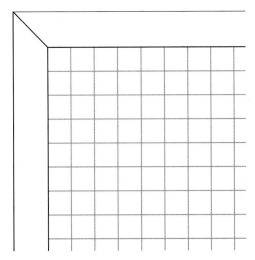

Mitered border

BORDER YARDAGE REQUIREMENTS

You must first determine the actual size of your quilt top. Do not use the sizes given with each quilt pattern since the slightest difference in seam allowances can alter this quilt size by as little as one fourth of an inch to as much as two or three inches. Begin by measuring your quilt top. Press the quilt top first, to make sure the quilt top is free from any creases and wrinkles. If possible, lay the quilt flat on a floor or table. For an accurate measurement, do not measure along the edges of the quilt, since they are easily stretched. Instead, measure through the center of the quilt from the top edge to the bottom edge for the length, and measure through the center of the quilt, from side to side, for the width.

For a sample guideline, we will use 62" width and 82" length. You must now determine the width of border to add. We will use a 4" finished width for the sample.

A 4" finished border will be cut 4½" (4" plus two seam allowances of ¼"). You will also want to decide on either a right angle border or a mitered border.

Figure the perimeter of the quilt top by adding the width twice to the length twice.
$$62" + 62" + 82" + 82" = 288"$$

For a right angle border, add the width of the unfinished border times four to this number.
$$4½" \times 4 = 18" + 288" = 306"$$

For a mitered border, add the width of the unfinished border times eight to this number plus an extra 8" for the angled seams.
$$4½" \times 8 = 36" + 288" + 8" = 332"$$

Divide this length by 42" to determine how many 4½" strips are needed.
$$306" \div 42" = 7.3 \text{ rounded up to 8 strips}$$
$$\text{or } 332" \div 42" = 7.9 \text{ rounded up to 8 strips}$$

Now multiply the number of strips by the unfinished width of the border to determine the yardage.
$$8 \times 4½" = 36"$$

As 36" is exactly one yard, you would want to purchase 1⅛ yards to allow for shrinkage and squaring up.

If you are adding two or more borders, be sure to allow for the widths of all preceding borders in your measurements when figuring the yardage of the second or third border.

Cut the number of strips needed for the border, trim off the selvages and seam together, end to end with a ¼" seam allowance. Press the seams open. From this long piece, cut the border lengths needed.

RIGHT ANGLE BORDERS

Cut the side borders to the actual quilt length. Fold each border in half and finger press a crease, or put a pin at the fold. Find the center of the quilt side. With right sides together and the edges even, pin the centers of the border and quilt side together. Pin the ends of the border to the corner of the quilt. Next, pin between the existing pins and distribute any fullness over the length of the quilt. Sew the border using a ¼" seam allowance. Press the seam toward the border. Add the other side border in the same manner.

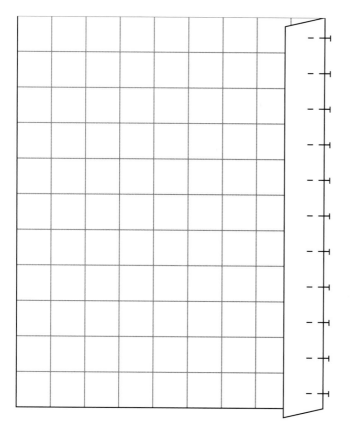

Before cutting the top and bottom borders to length, you must allow the extra width of the side borders. To your quilt width, add the width of the border twice, less 1" for seam allowances.

62" + (4½" x 2) = 71" - 1" = 70"

Cut the borders to this length. Find the center of the borders and the quilt top and bottom. Pin and sew the borders in the same manner as the side borders, matching the ends of the border to the corner of the side borders at each end. Press toward the border.

MITERED BORDERS

Measure the actual quilt length. For the side borders, add the length of the quilt to twice the width of the cut border plus 2" for the angled seam.

82" + (4½" x 2) = 91" + 2" = 93"

For the top and bottom borders, add the width of the quilt to twice the width of the cut border plus 2".

62" + (4½" x 2) = 71" + 2" = 73"

Starting with a side border, pin and sew one border at a time. Fold the border in half lengthwise and mark the center with a pin. From this pin measure toward the end to one half the actual length of your quilt.

82" ÷ 2 = 41"

Mark these spots with pins.

For the bottom border, find the center of your quilt edge (this can be done by counting squares), and pin the center of the border at this point. Align the pins near the ends of the border with the top and bottom edges of the quilt. Pin between the existing pins, easing in any fullness.

Start stitching at one corner of the quilt, with the border on the bottom and starting ¼" in from the raw edges of the quilt. Backstitch at the ends, but take care not to stitch into the ¼" seam allowance. Sew the length of the quilt, stopping stitching ¼" from the edge of the quilt, and then backstitch.

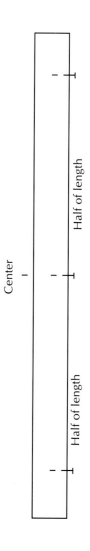

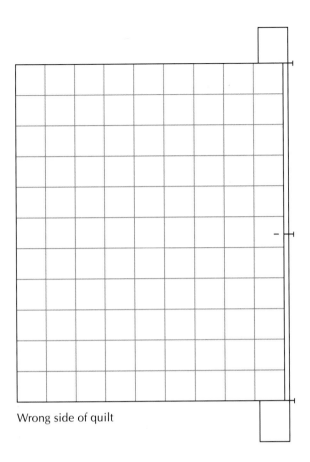

Wrong side of quilt

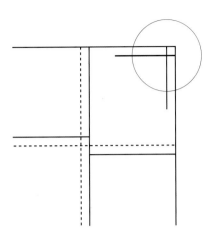

Helpful hint: Use a fabric pen or pencil and mark the ¼" seam allowances on the wrong side of the quilt, starting approximately 2" away from the corner and marking into the corner. The point at which these lines intersect is the starting and stopping points when sewing the borders.

Lay one corner of the quilt and border, right side up, on an ironing board. Open the border away from the quilt. Arrange the excess fabric of the borders to extend straight, lapping the vertical border over the horizontal border. Take the end of the vertical border and fold it under itself at a 45° angle, so the excess of this border is in line with the excess of the other border. Use a ruler with a 45° angle, and check that the angle is correct and the corner is square. Press this crease. Pin the excess of the borders together to hold the angle.

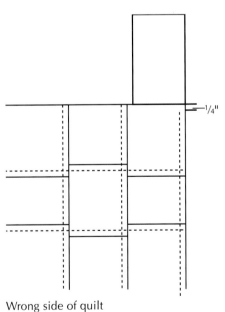

¼"

Wrong side of quilt

Add the second border. You will begin sewing at the point at which you stopped sewing on the previous border. Work around the quilt in this same manner to add the third and fourth border.

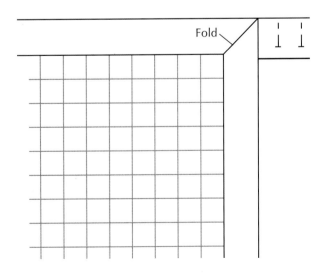

Fold

Pick up the quilt by the borders to allow the quilt to fold, right sides together, on the diagonal toward the corner of the quilt. Keep the raw edges of the borders even and sew at the crease of the border, starting at the outside of the borders and stitching toward the corner of the quilt. Stitch to the seam lines and then backstitch. Trim the seam allowance to ⅜" and press the seams open. Press the border seams toward the border.

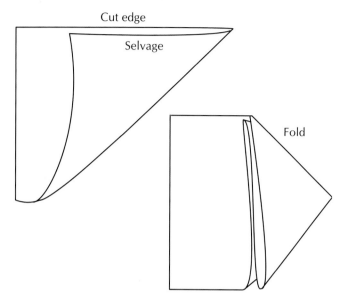

Wrong side of quilt

QUILTING YOUR QUILT

Most of the quilts in this book require simple straight line quilting, either in the ditch or at a diagonal line, that can be accomplished easily by either hand or machine. The Boston Commons and the Irish Chain quilts have plain areas where fancier designs and patterns fit nicely. These designs can also be hand or machine quilted. Although Blanche hand quilts when time allows, Dalene has only attempted to ply the needle by hand a few times and prefers to spend her time machine quilting. (Whether you chose to hand or machine quilt, we feel the directions needed for either of these methods would fill an entire book itself.) The Irish Chain quilt on page 101 was made and graciously loaned to us by Kaye Johnson, and machine quilted by Phyllis Reddish. The remaining quilts pictured in this book were made and machine quilted by the authors.

BINDING THE QUILT

The edges of a quilt receive the most wear and tear. With this in mind, we recommend a folded double binding for finishing the quilts. A bias binding is not necessary unless you are binding a curved edge or a quilt with inside corners such as the zig-zag edge of the Trip Around the World quilts.

To cut the strips for a bias binding, begin by squaring up the cut edges of your fabric. Now fold your fabric diagonally, bringing a selvage even with a cut edge, then fold again diagonally, as shown.

Cut edge

Selvage

Fold

Cut a straight line close to the fold, and then cut strips at 2¼" increments.

To cut the strips for a straight of grain binding, follow the steps in the Cutting Accurate Strips section on page 6 for cutting straight strips. Cut the selvages off with a 45° angle, as shown.

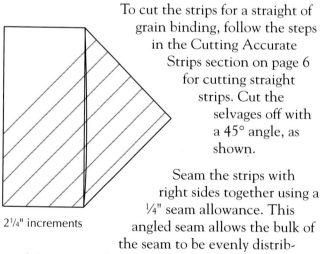

2¼" increments

Seam the strips with right sides together using a ¼" seam allowance. This angled seam allows the bulk of the seam to be evenly distributed. Lay one end of the seamed strips face down on an ironing surface, with the tip of the angle to the right. Press a ⅜" hem along the 45° angle. Recut the angle, if necessary.

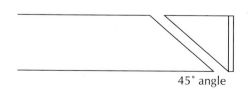

45° angle

Press the seam allowances open and then press the long strip in half lengthwise, with wrong sides together. To avoid ruffling when sewing the binding on, we recommend that you staystitch along the edge of the binding just short of a ¼" from the raw edges.

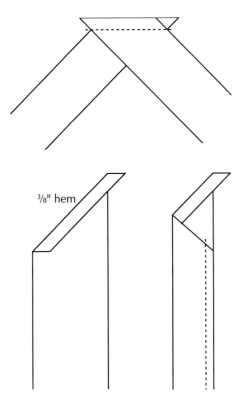

³/₈" hem

Working from the right side of the quilt, lay the binding on the quilt, lining up the raw edges of the quilt top to the raw edge of the binding. Sew just to the left of the line of staystitching, using a ¼" seam.

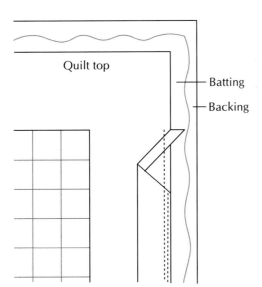

Quilt top

Batting

Backing

To turn the corners of the quilt, stop stitching ¼" from the end of the border, and then, without cutting your thread, lift the machine needle and pressure foot and move the quilt out from under the machine. Fold a ¼" pleat in the binding, and insert the needle on the other side of the pleat. Pivot the quilt with the needle down, backstitch to the folded edge of the pleat, and then continue sewing.

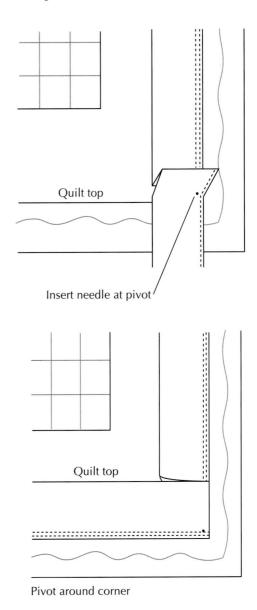

Quilt top

Insert needle at pivot

Quilt top

Pivot around corner

Sew around the quilt. When you reach the starting point, simply overlap the binding at least an inch past the folded hem of the beginning of the binding. Trim the backing and batting approximately ½" away from the binding seam line. This backing and batting will fill up the binding, which prevents wear along the outer fold.

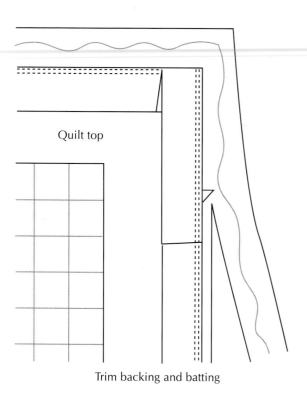

Quilt top

Trim backing and batting

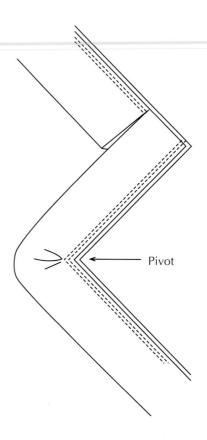

Pivot

Turn the bias binding over to the back of the quilt and blindstitch it to the backing. The seam lines will be hidden within the binding.

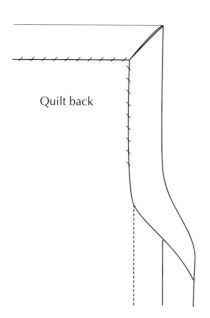

Quilt back

The binding for a Trip Around the World quilt is sewn on the same as a straight edge binding, except there are many more outside corners and the inside corners need to be pivoted around. To pivot around an inside corner, stop stitching ¼" from the two raw edges of the corner, and then with the needle down, pivot around the corner.

HELPFUL HINTS

It may seem that one of the most difficult steps in making some of the quilts in this book is keeping the correct order of the fabrics. However, all of the quilt patterns have numbers assigned to each fabric, so once you have selected the fabrics for your quilt and have decided on their placement in the quilt, just write the quilt name across the top of a piece of paper and list the fabric numbers in a column. Then cut swatches of the fabrics and pin, tape, or glue the swatches next to the corresponding numbers. Keep this paper nearby as you work, and if the directions call for you to cut six strips of Fabric 5, simply glance at your sheet of swatches to ensure you are cutting the right fabric.

After you have cut your strips and stacked them in the order they will be sewn into the sets, add a sticky note, or pin a small square of paper onto the top of the first strip in the pile (this should be the top strip in the strip set). Write the strip set letter, such as Strip Set A, B, or C, onto the paper. This will not only keep the strip sets organized, but will also help you keep track of the top fabric in the strip sets—which will also be the top fabric in the sections when they are cut. This is very important since some of the sections are turned upside down in the various quilt projects.

CHAPTER 2

SCRAP BOSTON COMMONS

◆

Twilight Comfort

PLANNED BOSTON COMMONS

Garden Trellis

SCRAP AND PLANNED BOSTON COMMONS
74" x 89" without second plain border
88" x 103" with 7" plain border
1¾" finished square

The Scrap Boston Commons and the Planned Boston Commons are essentially the same quilt. The two quilts are made employing the same techniques, with the exception of the yardage requirements and cutting and sewing the strips sets. Separate instructions are provided for the first steps of each quilt construction. Then, beginning with Cutting the Strip Sets into Sections, the instructions are combined for both quilts.

SCRAP BOSTON COMMONS

Fabric requirements for the patchwork center and borders: ¼ yard each of eight fabrics for each of the seven fabric groups. (¼ yard each of six fabrics for each of the seven fabric groups is sufficient, but we feel eight fabrics in each group gives a "scrappier" look to the quilt). The first Fabric Group A is the lightest color value and the second Fabric Group B is a darker value. Each fabric group will darken in color value to Group G, where the fabrics are the darkest color value. Refer to page 5 to review the suggestions on color values, if needed.

Fabric requirements for the plain borders: 1⅞ yards of a light value fabric for the first plain border, or 5 yards of a light value fabric for the first and second plain borders for a larger quilt.

Note: This is the only pattern in which we have used letters to identify the fabrics and numbers to identify the strip sets. We did this so that the actual number of fabrics used in a strip set matches the section number.

INSTRUCTIONS

Review the basic instructions starting on page 5, if needed.

Step 1. Separate the fabrics into seven groups of eight fabrics. Group A is the lightest and Group G is the darkest.

Step 2. For Fabric Group A, cut one 2¼" square from each of the eight fabrics. These will be Strip Set 1.

For Fabric Groups A through F, cut three 2¼" strips from each fabric to yield 24 strips per fabric group. Keeping each fabric group separate from the others, cut all the strips in half (these must be at least 20" long). Set aside twenty-four 20" strips from each fabric group (three from each individual fabric, if possible). These strips will be used in Strip Set 13. Cut the remaining strips in half again (these should be at least 10" long). These strips will be used in Strip Sets 2 through 12. Stack the strips in piles according to size and fabric group.

For Fabric Group G, cut two 2¼" strips from each of the eight fabrics. Cut the strips in half (at least 20" long). Set aside 12 of these strips to be used in Strip Set 13. Cut the remaining strips in half again (at least 10" long). These will be used in Strip Sets 7 through 12.

Step 3. Strip Set 1 isn't really a strip set at all since it consists only of the eight 2¼" squares cut from Fabric Group A.

For Strip Sets 2 through 12, sew the 10" strips together to construct the strip sets. Start with Strip Set 2. Select a 10" strip from Fabric Group B and lay it face up. Then select a 10" strip from Fabric Group A and lay it face down on top of the other strip. Stitch the strips together along the long edge. Fabric B is the top of this strip set, as shown. Always start with the top strip when sewing each strip set. Use the illustration as a guide to complete the strip sets. You will need two each of Strip Sets 2 through 11 and four of Strip Set 12. Notice that the strip set numbers correspond with the number of strips it contains.

For Strip Set 13, sew the 20" strips together in the same manner as the previous strip sets. You will need 12 of Strip Set 13.

Step 4. In each strip set, press the seam allowances in alternating directions toward Fabric Groups B, D, and F.

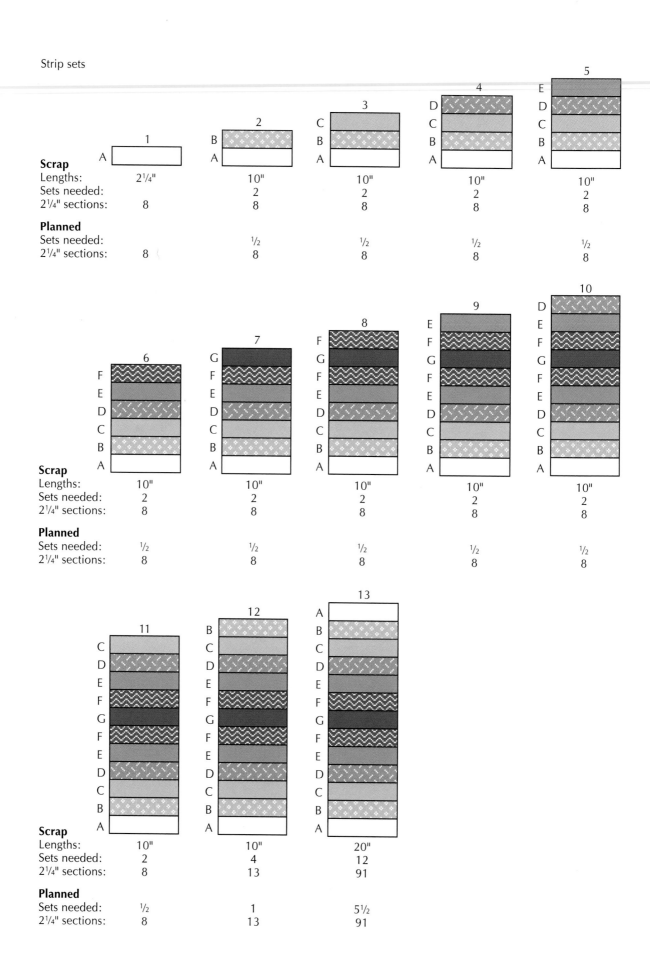

Scrap

	1	2	3	4	5
Lengths:	2¼"	10"	10"	10"	10"
Sets needed:		2	2	2	2
2¼" sections:	8	8	8	8	8

Planned

Sets needed:		½	½	½	½
2¼" sections:	8	8	8	8	8

Scrap

	6	7	8	9	10
Lengths:	10"	10"	10"	10"	10"
Sets needed:	2	2	2	2	2
2¼" sections:	8	8	8	8	8

Planned

Sets needed:	½	½	½	½	½
2¼" sections:	8	8	8	8	8

Scrap

	11	12	13
Lengths:	10"	10"	20"
Sets needed:	2	4	12
2¼" sections:	8	13	91

Planned

Sets needed:	½	1	5½
2¼" sections:	8	13	91

PLANNED BOSTON COMMONS

The Planned Boston Commons quilt differs from the Scrap Boston Commons quilt only in the number of fabrics used.

Fabric requirements: 1½ yards each of six fabrics for Fabrics A through F, ¾ yard of one fabric for Fabric G, 1⅛ yards of a light value fabric for the first plain border (the same fabric as Fabric A), or 5 yards of a light value fabric (the same fabric as Fabric A) for the first and second plain borders for a larger quilt. The color values should graduate from Fabric A, the lightest, to Fabric G, the darkest.

INSTRUCTIONS

Step 1. For Fabric A, cut eighteen 2¼" strips, and then cut six of these strips in half (at least 20" long). From one of these half strips, cut eight 2¼" squares. These squares are Strip Set 1.

For Fabrics B through F, cut eighteen 2¼" strips of each fabric. From each fabric, cut six of these strips in half (at least 20" long).

For Fabric G, cut nine 2¼" strips, and then cut three of these strips in half.

Step 2. Strip Set 1 isn't really a strip set at all since it consists only of eight 2¼" squares cut from Fabric A.

For Strip Sets 2 through 12, sew the half strips together to construct the strip sets. Start with Strip Set 2. Select a half strip from Fabric B and lay it face up. Then select a half strip from Fabric A and lay it face down on top of the other strip. Stitch the strips together along the long edge. Fabric B is the top of this strip set, as shown. Always start with the top strip when sewing each strip set. Use the illustration as a guide to complete the strip sets. You will need one half each of Strip Sets 2 through 11 and one of Strip Set 12. Notice that the strip set numbers correspond with the number of strips it contains.

For Strip Set 13, sew the whole strips together in the same manner as the previous strip sets. You will need five and a half of Strip Sets 13, so you will have one half strip set yet to sew together.

Step 3. In each strip set, press the seam allowances in alternating directions toward Fabrics B, D, and F.

COMBINED INSTRUCTIONS

Refer to the basic instructions starting on page 9 for stacking and cutting strip sets into sections, if needed.

Step 1. Cut the strip sets into sections or rows of squares. Lay each strip set face down and cut at 2¼" increments. Each 10" strip set will yield four sections, each 20" strip set will yield eight sections, and each whole strip set will yield 18 sections. Stack the cut sections into piles according to their section number.

Step 2. It is helpful at this time if you stack the cut sections in the order of their placement in the various units of the quilt. The center of the quilt is made of two corner units and five single rows. The borders are two side units and a top and bottom unit. Set aside five of Section 12 and five of Section 13 for the single rows in the center of the quilt. Stack the sections for the two corner units of the center of the quilt, face up, with the top edges of the sections even, in the following order: 1-2-3-4-5-6-7-8-9-10-11-12-13-12-11-10-9-8-7-6-5-4-3-2-1.

Notice that each section increases by one square to the center and then the sections decrease by one square. Make two stacks: one for each "corner" unit.

Step 3. Make two stacks for the side borders, face up, beginning with 23 of Section 13 in each pile and adding one of each section in the following order: 12-11-10-9-8-7-6-5-4-3-2-1.

Step 4. Make two stacks for the top and bottom borders, face up, beginning with 19 of Section 13 in each pile and adding one of each section in the following order: 12-11-10-9-8-7-6-5-4-3-2-1. Notice for the Scrap Boston Commons quilt that as you stack each Section 13 for the borders, you have 12 different sets of this section—so mix them up! Try to avoid identical sections being sewn next to each other.

Step 5. Leave the sections in the stacks face up. Pick up the first row, which will be a single square (Section 1), and lay it face up. Take the next section (Section 2) and place it face down on Section 1, keeping the top edges of the sections even. Stitch these sections together, using a scant ¼" seam allowance, and sew ¼" beyond the bottom edge of Section 1. Open the sections and place Section 3 face down on Section 2, taking care to keep the top edges even. Stitch Section 3 to Sections 2/1.

Continue adding sections in this manner. The pressed seam allowances will nest together to help create perfect corners.

Note that the bottom edge of the previous section always extends ¼" beyond the last seam in the section you are adding. This will be included in the seam allowance when the plain borders are added.

Step 6. In the completed center units, press the seam allowances in alternate directions toward Sections 2, 4, 6, 8, 10, and 12.

Step 7. To lengthen the center of the quilt, add single diagonal rows between the two diagonal center corner units (to complete the center of the quilt). These rows are offset by one square.

To construct the single rows, use one Section 12 and one Section 13. Sew the top of Section 12 to the bottom of Section 13. Make five single rows. To sew the single rows together to form the diagonal center of the quilt, simply offset the rows by one square. Continue sewing until all five rows are joined.

Add the completed center corner units to the single rows for the center patchwork section of the quilt. Press these last seams flat in any direction.

Note that the grain line of the single rows will run the opposite direction of the rows in the diagonal corner units. This will not be a problem unless you are using a one-way print or stripe. If a one-way print or a stripe is used, the single rows need to be constructed one square at a time to keep the direction of the prints in the single rows the same as the prints in the diagonal corners.

Step 8. Begin sewing the border units together in the same manner as the center corner units were constructed. Starting with your stacked piles facing down, add the single square (Section 1) facing up, and then place Section 2 face down over it keeping the top edges of the sections even. Stitch the sections together.

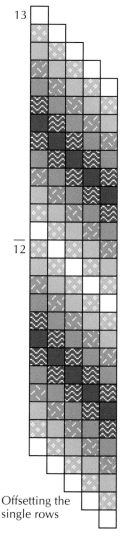

Offsetting the single rows

Add Section 3 to Sections 1/2, and continue in this manner until you have added the first Section 13. To add the remaining Sections 13, you must drop down or offset each row by one square. Press the seams in opposite directions, starting with the first seam pressed toward the center of the border piece.

Step 9. Sew the four border units together, as shown. Notice that the corners are formed with the outermost squares of the top and bottom borders.

Step 10. Not everyone sews the same width of a ¼" seam (most quilt sizes will vary within an inch or two), and this could cause problems when sewing on

Center corner unit

Section 1 2 3 4 5 6 7 8 9 10 11 12 13 12 11 10 9 8 7 6 5 4 3 2 1

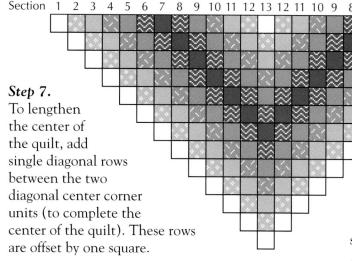

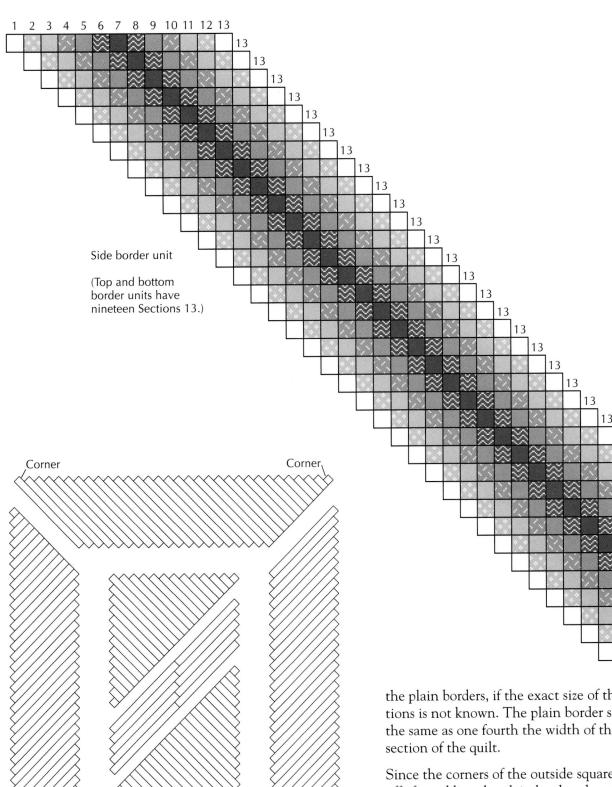

1 2 3 4 5 6 7 8 9 10 11 12 13

Side border unit

(Top and bottom border units have nineteen Sections 13.)

Corner Corner

Corner Corner

the plain borders, if the exact size of the sections is not known. The plain border should be the same as one fourth the width of the center section of the quilt.

Since the corners of the outside squares are cut off after adding the plain border, the quilt center is 12 squares wide. The plain borders should measure the same as three diagonal squares. Measure three diagonal squares in the center section, rather than multiplying the diagonal measurement of one square. Add ½" to the size for the seam allowance. The approximate cut width of the borders is 7½" to 8".

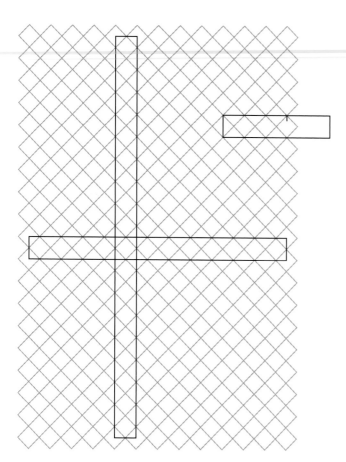

of squares around the center section will be trimmed off after the borders are added. You will be sewing through the diagonal center of these outside squares when adding the border. Fold the border in half lengthwise to find the center, and then place a pin at the center mark. Next, count the squares in your patchwork piece to find the center square. Pin the center of the border to the center of your patchwork, with right sides together. Pin the ends of the border through the miter crease and through the center of the last square. Pin the remainder of the border, distributing any fullness throughout the length of the patchwork piece.

Step 11. To determine the length of the top and bottom borders, measure across the middle width of the center section, starting from the tips of the second row of squares. To this measurement add the width of the border twice plus ½" for the seam allowance. For the side borders, measure across the middle length of the center section. To this measurement add twice the width of the borders plus ½" for the seam allowance.

Step 12. Cut the borders on the lengthwise grain of the fabric. Trim the selvages off the border fabric, and cut four lengthwise strips the desired width. Cut the borders to length. Fold and press the ends at a 45° angle, as shown. This crease will mark the miter seams.

← Crease   Crease →

Step 13. When sewing the borders onto the patchwork piece, you will be sewing on the bias of the pieced squares so caution must be taken to prevent stretching. Note that the extra fabric of the last row

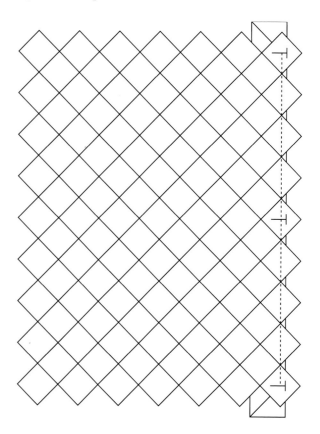

Position the border on the bottom, and use the edges or tips of the squares as a guide as to where to sew. Begin and end sewing at the pin that is through the center of the last square and the miter crease in the border. Stitch through the points of the outside squares. Pin and sew one border at a time. Trim the last row of squares even with the ¼" seam allowance of the border.

Step 14. Now that all four plain borders are added, you must now miter the corners. Simply align the miter creases, and then pin and sew. Sew from the outside of the border in toward the patchwork center. Trim the excess fabric and press the seams open.

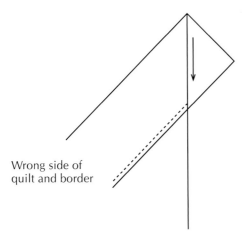

Wrong side of
quilt and border

Step 15. Before adding the patchwork borders, you need to prepare the four inside corners of the borders. The extending stitches need to be removed so that the seam ends on the sewing line of the square. Remove the stitches and backstitch on the sewing line of the square.

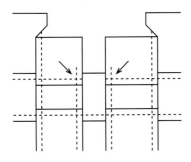

Step 16. Fold the corners of the plain border until the fold measures the same amount as the square plus the seam allowances. Crease this fold line.

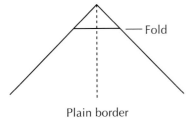

— Fold

Plain border

Step 17. Pin the four inside corners of the patchwork border to the corners of the plain borders, matching the crease and the sewing line of the square. Sew from seam line to seam line.

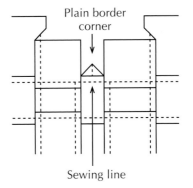

Plain border corner

Sewing line

Step 18. Pin the length of the borders together (one side at a time), starting in the center and working toward the ends while easing in any fullness. Sew with the plain border on the bottom and the patchwork on top. Begin and end the stitching at the point of the corner seams, and use the points or tips of the squares as a guide as to where to sew. Trim the extra fabric (the "ears" of the squares) even with the border seam allowance. Press the seam allowances toward the plain borders.

Step 19. If you are adding a second plain border to increase the size of the quilt, measure through the center of the quilt, top to bottom and side to side, to determine the length and width of the quilt. To these measurements add the width of the border twice plus ½" for the seam allowance. Cut the borders and fold the miter crease. Add this border as you did the first plain border. Trim the extra fabric (or "ears") even with the border seam allowance.

BABY BOSTON COMMONS

Mayflowers

Katherine's Quilt

BABY BOSTON COMMONS
43" x 48" without second plain border
1½" finished square

Fabric requirements: ⅝ yard each of four Fabrics A through D, ⅜ yard of Fabric E, and one yard of a plain border fabric (the same fabric as Fabric A) for a total of five fabrics graduating in color value from Fabric A, the lightest, to Fabric E, the darkest.

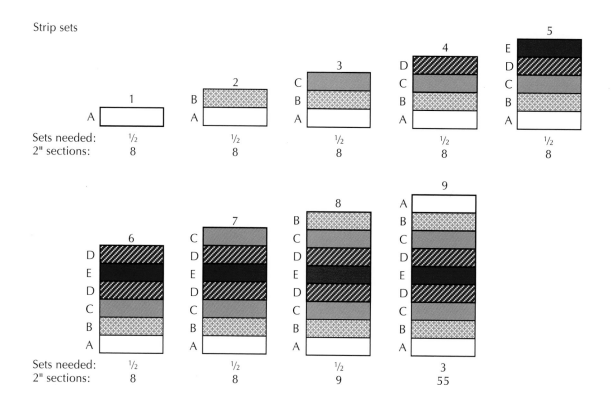

Strip sets

	1	2	3	4	5
Sets needed:	½	½	½	½	½
2" sections:	8	8	8	8	8

	6	7	8	9
Sets needed:	½	½	½	3
2" sections:	8	8	9	55

INSTRUCTIONS

Refer to the Boston Commons instructions starting on page 19, if needed.

Step 1. For Fabrics A, B, C, and D, cut ten 2" strips of each fabric. From these strips, cut four strips of each fabric in half to yield eight half strips. For Fabric E, cut five 24" strips. From these strips, cut two strips in half to yield four half strips.

Step 2. Strip Set 1 isn't really a strip set at all, it is a single half strip. Cut this strip into eight 2" squares. For Strip Sets 2 through 8, sew the half strips sets together in the order shown, always beginning with the top strip. Sew the strips together with a scant ¼" seam allowance. Make each strip set 21" long (half strip). For Strip Set 9, sew the strips together in the order shown. Make three full sets of Strip Set 9. Sew

the strips together with a scant ¼" seam allowance. Press the seam allowances in the strip sets toward Fabrics B and D.

Step 3. Cut the strip sets into sections at 2" increments. Cut the needed number of each section. Set aside one Section 8 and one Section 9 for the single row.

Step 4. Stack the sections needed for the two diagonal corners. Keeping the top edges of the sections even, stack the sections face up. Stack two piles in the following order: 1-2-3-4-5-6-7-8-9-8-7-6-5-4-3-2-1. Stack the sections for the four border units, making one stack for each unit. Stack the sections, face up, beginning with thirteen of Section 9 and adding one of each section in the following order: 8-7-6-5-4-3-2-1.

Step 5. Sew the sections together in the order stacked. Beginning with the single square of Section 1 (Fabric A), place the fabric face up and lay Section 2, face down, atop Section 1, keeping the top edges even. Stitch the sections together, using a scant ¼" seam allowance and sewing ¼" beyond the end of Section 1. Open the two sections and add a Section 3 on top of Section 2, sewing ¼" beyond the end of Section 2. Notice how each section increases by one square, up to the center row (Section 9), and then the rows decrease by one square to the single square of Section 1. Continue adding the sections in this manner to complete the two diagonal center corners. Press the seams in the completed center corner units toward Sections 2, 4, 6, and 8.

Step 6. To lengthen the center of the quilt, add a single diagonal row between the two diagonal center corner units (to complete the center of the quilt). This row is made of one Section 8 and one Section 9 by sewing the top of Section 8 to the bottom of Section 9.

Step 7. Sew the four border units together. Begin sewing the border units in the same manner as the diagonal corners. Start with Section 1 and add Section 2, and then add Section 3. The rows will increase in length by one square up to Section 9. After the first Section 9 is added, each Section 9 is dropped down or offset by one square as shown. Complete four border units. Press the seams in the border units in alternate directions, beginning with the first seam pressed toward the center of the border unit.

Step 8. Not everyone sews the same width of a ¼" seam (most quilt sizes vary within an inch or two) and this could cause problems when sewing on the plain borders if the

exact size of the sections is not known. The plain border should be the same size as one fourth the width of the center section of the quilt.

Since the corners of the outside squares are cut off after adding the plain border, the quilt center is eight squares wide. The plain borders should measure the same as two diagonal squares. Measure the two diagonal squares in the center section, rather than multiplying the diagonal measurement of one square. Add ½" to the size for the seam allowance. The approximate width of the borders is 4½".

Step 9. To determine the length of the borders, refer to Step 11 of the Boston Commons instructions on page 24.

Step 10. To complete the quilt, refer to Steps 12–18 of the Boston Commons instructions on pages 24–25.

CHAPTER 3

MANY TRIPS AROUND THE WORLD
BASIC INSTRUCTIONS

The construction of the Many Trips Around the World quilts, with their different variations, are basically the same. The differences in the variations are in the widths of the strips and the sections, the number of fabrics used for each, and the placement of the fabrics in the quilt design. The instructions for each quilt begins with the cut strips being sewn into strips sets, and then the strip sets being cut into sections. The sections are then sewn into units the width of the quilt and joined together with horizontal rows of single squares to complete the quilt top.

CUTTING THE STRIPS

Review the basic instructions starting on page 6 for cutting accurate strips. Cut the number of strips needed from each fabric. Be sure to cut the correct width of strips for the quilt you have chosen to make.

STACKING THE STRIPS

We find it very useful to stack the strips in the order they will be sewn into the strip sets. For example, Strip Set A of the large Many Trips Around the World quilt requires Fabrics 2, 3, 4, 5, and 6. Leave the strips folded in fourths and stack the strips starting with the bottom of the strip set, Fabric 6, and then add Fabric 5 to the pile, then Fabric 4, *etc.* If some of the designs call for half a strip set, simply cut the needed strips in half before stacking. Keep the strips in the order in which they will be sewn together. (Note that the strip at the top of each pile will be the top fabric in the sections that are later cut from these strip sets.) You will not use all of the strips at first, so don't be alarmed when you have leftover strips. Set aside the remaining strips to cut into single squares to make single square units.

SEWING THE STRIP SETS

Review the basic instruction starting on page 8 for sewing and pressing the strip sets.

STACKING AND CUTTING THE STRIP SETS INTO SECTIONS

The strip sets are now cut into sections. The width of these sections will be the same width as you originally cut the strips (except for the Many Extended Trips Around the World quilt). Review the basic instructions starting on page 9 for stacking and cutting strip sets into sections.

STACKING THE CUT SECTIONS

You will now have either four, six, or seven stacks of cut sections depending on which quilt you are making. Line the strips up in the following order: A, B, C, *etc.* Be sure that the top fabric of each section is in the same position in this line. This is very important as the sections are reversed throughout the units in some of the quilts. You now want to stack the sections in the order they will be sewn into the units. With the exception of the baby quilts, the Original Many Trips, and Many Extended Trips (which all have four main units), all of the Many Trips quilts require eight main units.

SEWING THE UNITS

Now that all of the sections are stacked, you can begin sewing the main units together. To facilitate construction of the Unit I, we use chain piecing. Take the first section of the unit and lay it face up on your machine. Then take the next section (which will be the second section of the unit) and place it face down on top of the first section. Sew these two sections together. Without clipping your threads, repeat this step with the seven (or three) remaining pairs of sections. Bring the first unit around and add the third sections. Continue adding the sections to each main unit. Press the seam allowances as directed in the quilt instructions.

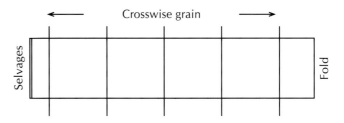

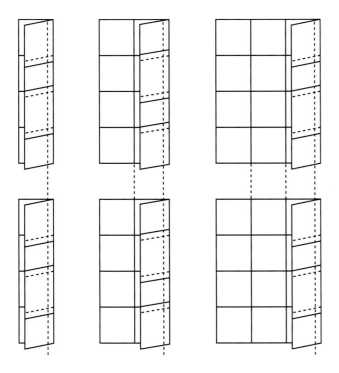

SINGLE SQUARE UNITS

To complete the design of the Many Trips quilts, rows of single squares need to be constructed. The crosswise grain of fabric is across the width of the units. Since the crosswise grain of fabric has a little stretch in it, it is very helpful to have the crosswise grain of the fabric across the width of the rows, when sewing the main unit and the single rows together. This will allow you to ease the corners together to match perfectly. Using the remaining strips, cut the number of single squares needed for each fabric. These squares are cut the same size as the strips (if your strips are cut 2½", your squares will be 2½"—except for Many Extended Trips, which are cut 2½" x 3¼"). Lay your strips folded in half horizontally across your cutting mat. You can stack two or three strips at a time. As you cut the squares, stack them in a pile without turning them, keeping the crosswise grain in the same direction. (Place a straight pin in the top square that points in the direction of the crosswise grain to help avoid confusion.)

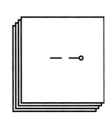

If you are unsure of the crosswise grain after the squares are cut, take one square and hold it between your thumb and index finger of both hands, and tug gently. The lengthwise grain is taut without any give, and the crosswise grain stretches a little. When sewing together the single rows, always keep the crosswise grain horizontal. You will be sewing along the lengthwise grain of the fabric when joining the single squares.

The single square rows can be constructed either one at a time or chain pieced together. We prefer chain piecing, and, of course, we start with stacking the squares in the order they will be sewn. Five of Single Square Unit II are needed and four of Single Square Unit III are needed, with the exception of the baby quilts, the Original Many Trips, and the Many Extended Trips, which need three Single Square Units II and two Single Square Units III. We stack the single squares just as we stacked the cut sections for the main units. As in the main unit, the single rows, if folded in half, are mirror images of each other while the center square divides the two halves.

STACKING THE SINGLE SQUARES

To stack the squares for Single Square Unit II, follow the chart in the specific quilt instructions. Count out five single squares of the first fabric in the single row and lay them down, keeping track of the crosswise grain. Count out five squares of the second fabric in the single row, and place them in another stack, keeping the crosswise grain in the same direction as the first squares. Continue stacking the squares in the order they will be sewn. Repeat the process for the four Single Square Units III, but stack groups of four instead of five.

SEWING THE SINGLE SQUARE UNITS

To chain piece the single rows, start with the five top squares of the first Single Square Unit II pile, laying them down and placing the first square face up on your machine. (Check that the crosswise grain is horizontal and that you will be sewing along the lengthwise grain). Take the first square off the top of the second pile (the second square of the single row), and place it face down on top of the first. Sew the two squares together for the rest of Units II, and then start back at the first row and add the third square of the single row to all the rows. Continue chain piecing the five Single Square Units II and four Single Square Units III. Press the seam allowances in the directions required in the quilt pattern.

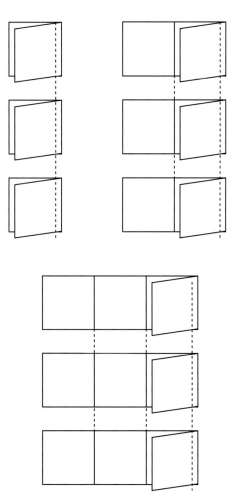

JOINING THE UNITS

You now have eight Units I, five Single Square Units II, and four Single Square Units III (or four Units I, three Single Square Units II, and two Single Square Units III). Sew these units together across the width of the quilt top. The seam allowances are pressed in alternating directions which will allow the seams to nest together. Since you will be sewing along the crosswise grain, there is a little give in the fabric, if needed, to make the corners intersect evenly. Notice that Unit I is turned upside down the second, fourth, sixth, and eighth time it is used.

It is very helpful at this time, to lay out the units in the order they will be sewn. Lay a Single Square Unit II, face up, in your machine and place the top edge of a Unit I, face down, on top of the first unit. Sew these two units together. Open these two units and sew a Single Square Unit III to the bottom of the Unit I. Next, add a Unit I that's been turned upside down (you will be sewing on the bottom edge of Unit I). Continue adding the units in this order for three more times. The final row added will be a Single Square Unit II. Press these final seams as directed in the individual quilt instructions. Add the borders, if desired, following the instructions starting on page 10.

ORIGINAL MANY TRIPS AROUND THE WORLD

Grande Nosegay

Sapphire Sea

Both of these quilts contain ten fabrics. They are essentially the same design, but the Many Extended Trips quilt squares differ in that they are ¾" longer than they are wide, which results in a quilt top that is longer than it is wide. The Original Many Trips quilt squares are 2" square, which results in a square quilt.

The construction steps are the same for both quilts, except for the width the strips are cut. The Original Many Trips quilt requires 2½" strips and the Many Extended quilt requires 3¼" strips. Once these strips are cut, the quilts are assembled in the same manner. The strip sets and units are identical.

ORIGINAL MANY TRIPS AROUND THE WORLD
74" x 74" without borders
2" finished square

FABRIC #	YARDAGE	2½" STRIPS	2½" SQUARES*
1	⅛ yard	1	13
2	¼ yard	3	20
3	⅜ yard	5	20
4	⅝ yard	7	20
5	¾ yard	9	20
6	⅞ yard	11	20
7	1 yard	13	20
8	1⅛ yards	15	20
9	1¼ yards	17	20
10	¾ yard	9	12

MANY EXTENDED TRIPS AROUND THE WORLD
74" x 101¾" without borders
2¾" x 2" finished square

FABRIC#	YARDAGE	3¼" STRIPS	3¼" X 2½" RECTANGLES*
1	⅛ yard	1	13
2	⅓ yard	3	20
3	½ yard	5	20
4	⅔ yard	7	20
5	1 yard	9	20
6	1⅛ yards	11	20
7	1¼ yards	13	20
8	1½ yards	15	20
9	1⅝ yards	17	20
10	1 yard	9	12

*The single squares are cut, at a later step, from the strips remaining after sewing the strip sets.

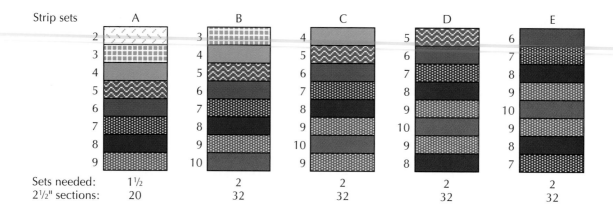

Strip sets	A	B	C	D	E
	2	3	4	5	6
	3	4	5	6	7
	4	5	6	7	8
	5	6	7	8	9
	6	7	8	9	10
	7	8	9	10	9
	8	9	10	9	8
	9	10	9	8	7
Sets needed:	1½	2	2	2	2
2½" sections:	20	32	32	32	32

Unit I
Make four

A B C D E E D C B A B C D E E D C B A B C D E E D C B A B C D E E D C B A

Single Square Unit II
Make three

1 2 3 4 5 6 7 8 9 10 9 8 7 6 5 4 3 2 1 2 3 4 5 6 7 8 9 10 9 8 7 6 5 4 3 2 1

Single Square Unit III
Make two

10 9 8 7 6 5 4 3 2 1 2 3 4 5 6 7 8 9 10 9 8 7 6 5 4 3 2 1 2 3 4 5 6 7 8 9 10

INSTRUCTIONS

Refer to the Many Trips Around the World basic instructions starting on page 30, if needed.

Step 1. For the Original Many Trips, cut the required number of 2½" strips needed from each fabric. For the Many Extended Trips, cut the required number of 3¼" strips needed from each fabric.

Step 2. Stack the strips needed for each strip set. When a half strip set is required, simply cut the strips in half. Set aside the remaining strips so they can be later cut into 2½" single squares.

Step 3. Sew the required number of strip sets.

Step 4. Press the seam allowances toward the even-numbered fabrics in each strip set.

Step 5. For both the Original Many Trips and the Many Extended Trips, stack and cut the strip sets into 2½" sections.

Step 6. Sew the sections together into units. Make four of Unit I.

Step 7. Press the seams of two Units I to the right. Press the seams of the remaining two Units I to the left.

Step 8. Using the remaining strips that were set aside in Step 2, cut the required number of single blocks from each fabric. The Original Many Trips requires 2½" squares. The Many Extended Trips requires 3¼" x 2½" rectangles.

Step 9. Sew the single squares together to form the Single Square Units II and III. Three of Single Square Unit II are needed and two of Single Square Unit III are needed. When sewing the squares together, take care to keep the crosswise

grain running across the units. The crosswise grain of the Many Extended Trips single rectangles are across the 2½" width of the rectangles, so you will need to sew along the longer edge when joining the single rectangles.

Step 10. Press all the seam allowances of the sewn squares or rectangles to the left.

Step 11. Lay the units together so the pressed seam allowances will nest together at each seam line. Sew the units together in the order shown.

Step 12. Refer to the instructions starting on page 10 for adding borders, if desired.

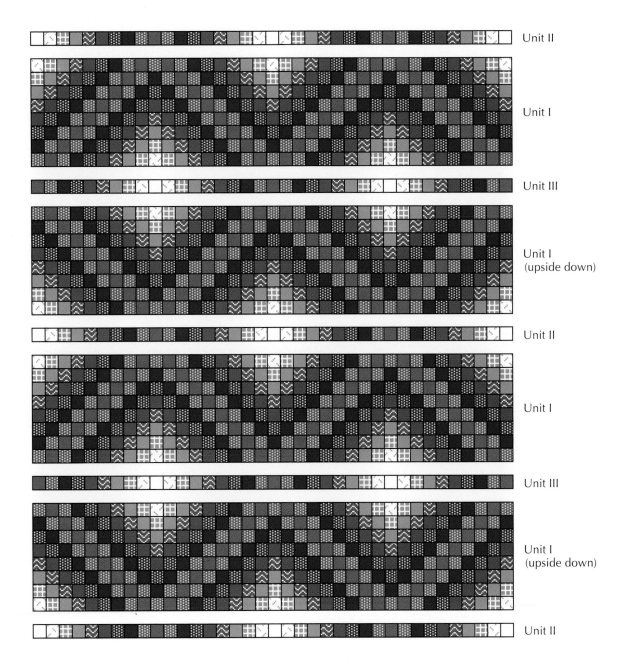

Unit II

Unit I

Unit III

Unit I (upside down)

Unit II

Unit I

Unit III

Unit I (upside down)

Unit II

REGULAR MANY TRIPS AROUND THE WORLD

Pacific Tranquility

REGULAR MANY TRIPS AROUND THE WORLD
74" x 98" without borders
2" finished square

This version of the Many Trips Around the World quilt repeats the same fabric sequence throughout the quilt. Using seven different fabrics together makes a beautiful traditional quilt. The first fabric is the center of each Trip (usually the lightest value fabric). The seventh fabric is the chain or connecting fabric between each Trip (the darkest).

FABRIC #	YARDAGE	2½" STRIPS	2½" SQUARES
1	¼ yard	2	32
2	⅝ yard	7	54
3	1 yard	13	54
4	1½ yards	19	54
5	1⅞ yards	25	54
6	2¼ yards	31	54
7	1¼ yards	17	31

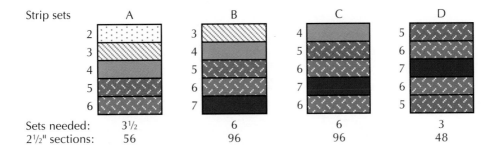

Strip sets

	A	B	C	D
	2 3 4 5 6	3 4 5 6 7	4 5 6 7 6	5 6 7 6 5
Sets needed:	3½	6	6	3
2½" sections:	56	96	96	48

Unit I—Make eight

A B C D C B A B C D C B A B C D C B A B C D C B A B C D C B A B C D C B A B C D C B A

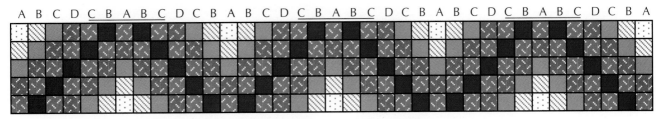

The underlined sections need to be turned upside down before sewing into Units I.

Single Square Unit II—Make five

1 2 3 4 5 6 7 6 5 4 3 2 1 2 3 4 5 6 7 6 5 4 3 2 1 2 3 4 5 6 7 6 5 4 3 2 1

Single Square Unit III—Make four

7 6 5 4 3 2 1 2 3 4 5 6 7 6 5 4 3 2 1 2 3 4 5 6 7 6 5 4 3 2 1 2 3 4 5 6 7

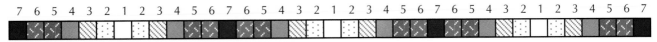

INSTRUCTIONS

Refer to the Many Trips Around the World basic instructions starting on page 30, if needed.

Step 1. Cut the required number of 2½" strips needed from each fabric.

Step 2. Stack the strips needed for each strip set. When a half strip set is required, simply cut the full strips in half. Set aside the remaining strips to be cut later into single squares.

Step 3. Sew the required number of strip sets.

Step 4. Press the seam allowances toward the even-numbered fabrics in each strip set.

Step 5. Stack and cut the strips sets into 2½" sections.

Step 6. Sew the sections together to form Unit I. Make eight of Unit I. Note that throughout the unit some of the sections are turned upside down.

Step 7. Press the seam allowances of four Units I to the right and four Units I to the left.

Step 8. Using the remaining strips that were set aside in Step 2, cut the required number of 2½" single squares from each fabric.

Step 9. Sew the single squares together to form Single Square Units II and

III. Five of Single Square Units II are needed and four of Single Square Units III are needed.

Step 10. Press all the seam allowances to the right.

Step 11. Lay the units together so the pressed seam allowances will nest together at each seam line. Sew the units together in the order shown.

Step 12. Refer to the instructions starting on page 10 for adding borders, if desired.

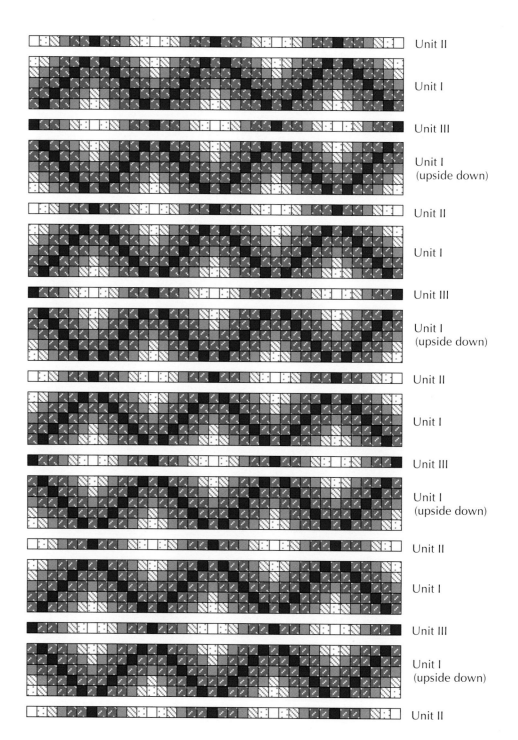

Unit II

Unit I

Unit III

Unit I
(upside down)

Unit II

Unit I

Unit III

Unit I
(upside down)

Unit II

Unit I

Unit III

Unit I
(upside down)

Unit II

Unit I

Unit III

Unit I
(upside down)

Unit II

BABY
REGULAR MANY TRIPS AROUND THE WORLD

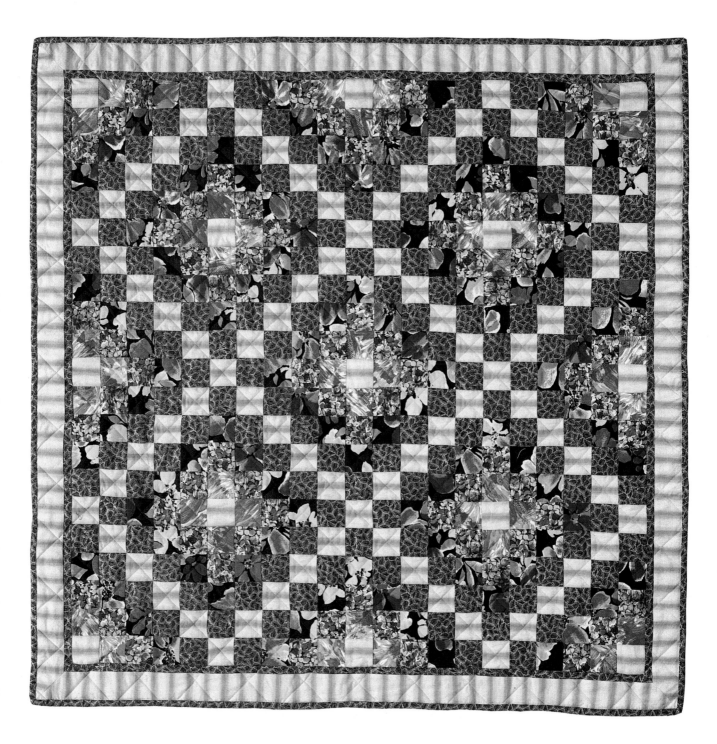

Gala

BABY
REGULAR MANY TRIPS AROUND THE WORLD

Easy Trip

BABY REGULAR MANY TRIPS AROUND THE WORLD
42" x 42" without borders
2" finished square

Fabric 1, the lightest, is the center square of each of the Mini Trip sections within the quilt. Fabric 6, the darkest, is the connecting fabric or chain between the Mini Trip sections.

FABRIC #	YARDAGE	2½" STRIPS	2½" SQUARES
1	⅛ yard	1	13
2	¼ yard	3	20
3	½ yard	5	20
4	⅝ yard	7	20
5	¾ yard	9	20
6	½ yard	5	12

Strip sets

	A	B	C
	2 3 4 5	3 4 5 6	4 5 6 5

Sets needed: 1½   2   2
2½" sections: 20   32   32

Unit I
Make four

A B C C B A B C C B A B C C B A B C C B A

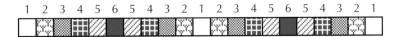

The underlined sections need to be turned upside down before sewing into Unit I.

Single Square Unit II
Make three

1 2 3 4 5 6 5 4 3 2 1 2 3 4 5 6 5 4 3 2 1

Single Square Unit III
Make two

6 5 4 3 2 1 2 3 4 5 6 5 4 3 2 1 2 3 4 5 6

INSTRUCTIONS

Refer to the Many Trips Around the World basic instructions starting on page 30, if needed.

Step 1. Cut the required number of 2½" strips needed from each fabric.

Step 2. Stack the strips needed for each strip set. When a half strip set is required, simply cut the full strips in half. Set aside the remaining strips to be cut later into single squares.

Step 3. Sew the required amount of strips sets.

Step 4. Press the seam allowances toward the even-numbered fabrics in each strip set.

Step 5. Stack and cut the strip sets into 2½" sections.

Step 6. Sew the sections together to form Unit I. Make four of Unit I. Note that throughout the unit some of the sections are turned upside down.

Step 7. Press the seam allowances of two of Unit I to the right and two of Unit I to the left.

Step 8. Using the remaining strips that were set aside in Step 2, cut the required number of 2½" single squares from each fabric.

Step 9. Sew the single squares together to form Single Square Units II and III. Three of Single Square Units II are needed and two of Single Square Units III are needed.

Step 10. Press all the seam allowances to the right.

Step 11. Lay the units together so the pressed seam allowances will nest together at each seam line. Sew the units together in the order shown.

Step 12. Refer to the instructions starting on page 10 for adding borders, if desired.

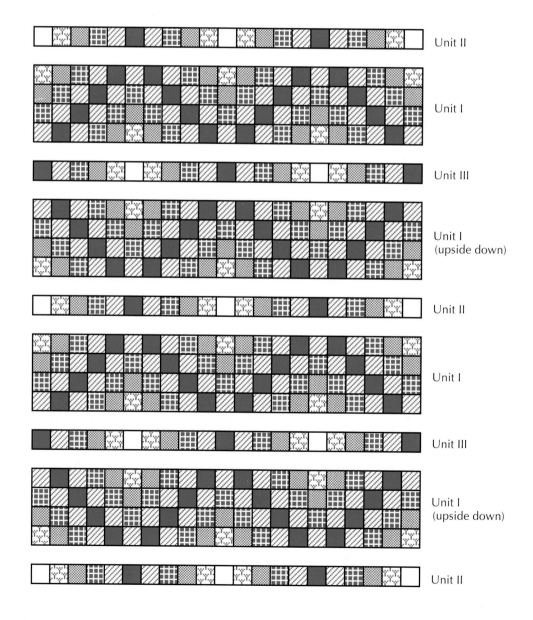

Unit II

Unit I

Unit III

Unit I
(upside down)

Unit II

Unit I

Unit III

Unit I
(upside down)

Unit II

'ROUND ABOUT THE WORLD

Fiesta

'ROUND ABOUT THE WORLD
74" x 98" without borders
2" finished square

This variation of The Many Trips Around the World reverses the fabric sequence within every other Trip section. When using fabrics ranging in value from light to dark (from Fabric 1 through 7), every other small Trip is light (Fabric 1) in the center graduating to dark. The other small Trips are dark (Fabric 6) in the center graduating to light. Fabric 7 is the connecting chain between each small Trip. Notice that in the reverse Trips, Fabric 1 is next to Fabric 7.

FABRIC #	YARDAGE	2½" STRIPS	2½" SQUARES
1	1⅜ yards	17	44
2	1¼ yards	16	54
3	1¼ yards	16	54
4	1¼ yards	16	54
5	1¼ yards	16	54
6	1⅜ yards	17	42
7	1⅜ yards	17	31

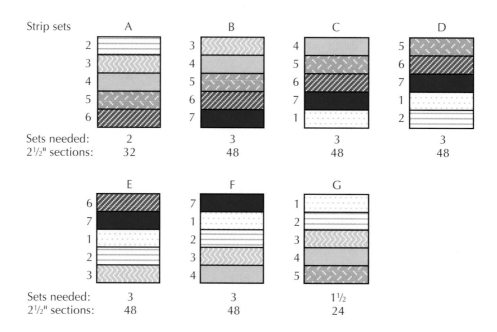

Unit I
Make eight

A B C D E F G F E D C B A B C D E F G F E D C B A B C D E F G F E D C B A

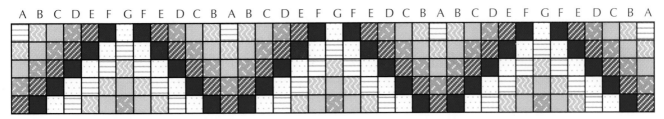

Single Square Unit II
Make five

1 2 3 4 5 6 7 6 5 4 3 2 1 2 3 4 5 6 7 6 5 4 3 2 1 2 3 4 5 6 7 6 5 4 3 2 1

Single Square Unit III
Make four

7 1 2 3 4 5 6 5 4 3 2 1 7 1 2 3 4 5 6 5 4 3 2 1 7 1 2 3 4 5 6 5 4 3 2 1 7

INSTRUCTIONS

Refer to the Many Trips Around the World basic instructions starting on page 30, if needed.

Step 1. Cut the required number of 2½" strips needed from each fabric.

Step 2. Stack the strips needed for each strip set. When a half strip set is required, simply cut the full strips in half. Set aside the remaining strips to be cut later into single squares.

Step 3. Sew the required number of strip sets.

Step 4. Press the seam allowances of the strip sets in the following directions: Strip Set A press toward Fabrics 2, 4, and 6; Strip Set B press toward Fabrics 4 and 6; Strip Set C press toward Fabrics 4, 6, and 1; Strip Set D press toward Fabrics 6 and 1; Strip Set E press toward Fabrics 6, 1, and 3; Strip Set F press toward Fabrics 1 and 3; and Strip Set G press toward Fabrics 1, 3, and 5. The seam allowances will alternate directions throughout the strip sets.

Step 5. Stack and cut the strip sets into 2½" sections.

Step 6. Sew the sections together to form Unit I. Make eight of Unit I.

Step 7. Press the seam allowances of four Units I to the right and four Units I to the left.

Step 8. Using the remaining strips that were set aside in step 2, cut the required number of 2½" single squares from each fabric.

Step 9. Sew the single squares together to form Single Square Units II and III. Five of Single Square Units II are needed and four of Single Square Units III are needed.

Step 10. Press all the seam allowances of the single square units to the right.

Step 11. Lay the units together so the pressed seam allowances will nest together at each seam line. Sew the units together in the order shown.

Step 12. Refer to the instructions starting on page 10 for adding borders, if desired.

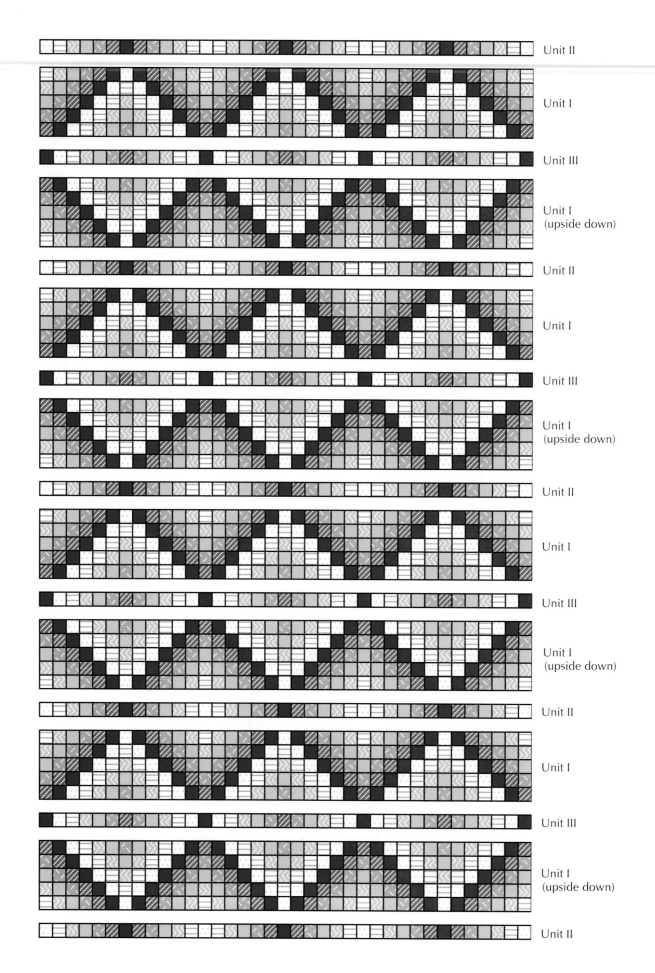

Unit II

Unit I

Unit III

Unit I
(upside down)

Unit II

Unit I

Unit III

Unit I
(upside down)

Unit II

Unit I

Unit III

Unit I
(upside down)

Unit II

Unit I

Unit III

Unit I
(upside down)

Unit II

BABY/WALL
'ROUND ABOUT THE WORLD

◆

Hopscotch; fabrics courtesy of P&B Textiles

BABY/WALL 'ROUND ABOUT THE WORLD
42" x 42" without borders
2" finished square

For the reverse design in *Hopscotch*, Fabric 1, the lightest, and Fabric 5, which is darker, are center squares in the Mini Trip sections. Fabric 6, the darkest, is the connecting chain between the Trips. The quilt uses a red fabric print as the connecting chain.

FABRIC #	YARDAGE	2½" STRIPS	2½" SQUARES
1	½ yard	5	17
2	½ yard	5	20
3	½ yard	5	20
4	½ yard	5	20
5	½ yard	5	16
6	½ yard	5	12

Strip sets

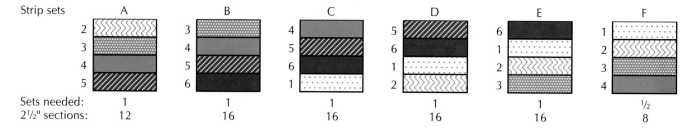

	A	B	C	D	E	F
Sets needed:	1	1	1	1	1	½
2½" sections:	12	16	16	16	16	8

Unit I
Make four

A B C D E F E D C B A B C D E F E D C B A

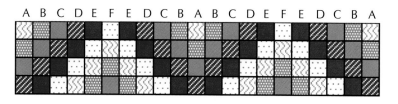

Single Square Unit II
Make three

1 2 3 4 5 6 5 4 3 2 1 2 3 4 5 6 5 4 3 2 1

Single Square Unit III
Make two

6 1 2 3 4 5 4 3 2 1 6 1 2 3 4 5 4 3 2 1 6

INSTRUCTIONS

Refer to the Many Trips Around the World basic instructions starting on page 30, if needed.

Step 1. Cut five 2½" strips from each fabric.

Step 2. Stack the strips needed for each strip set. When a half strip set is required, simply cut the full strips in half. Set aside the remaining strips to be cut later into single squares.

Step 3. Sew the required number of strip sets.

Step 4. Press the seam allowances toward the even-numbered fabrics in each strip set.

Step 5. Stack and cut the strip sets into 2½" sections.

Step 6. Sew the sections together to form Unit I. Make four of Unit I.

Step 7. Press the seam allowances of two Units I to the right and two Units I to the left.

Step 8. Using the remaining strips that were set aside in Step 2, cut the required number of 2½" single squares from each fabric.

Step 9. Sew the single squares together to form Single Square Units II and III. Three of Single Square Units II are needed and two of Single Square Units III are needed.

Step 10. Press all the seam allowances to the right.

Step 11. Lay the units together so the pressed seam allowances will nest together at each seam line. Join the units together in the order shown.

Step 12. Refer to the instructions starting on page 10 for adding borders, if desired.

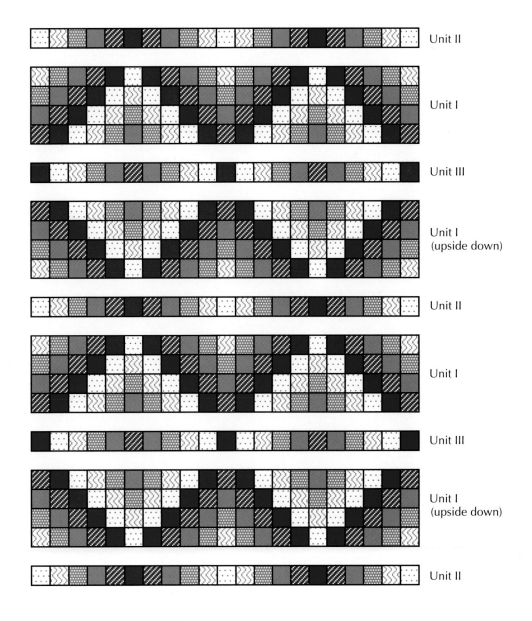

Unit II

Unit I

Unit III

Unit I
(upside down)

Unit II

Unit I

Unit III

Unit I
(upside down)

Unit II

SO MANY TRIPS AROUND THE WORLD

Tropical Trips

SO MANY TRIPS AROUND THE WORLD
77½" x 102½" without borders
2½" finished square

This variation of the Many Trips Around the World quilt is a sparkling design, reminiscent of an Irish Chain quilt. There are eleven fabrics used in the design. Fabrics 1 through 5 are of one color family, with Fabric 1 being the lightest color value and Fabric 5 being the darkest. Fabrics 6 through 10 are of another color family, with Fabric 6 being the lightest color value and Fabric 10 being the darkest. Fabric 0 is the connecting fabric, or chain, between the two fabrics.

FABRIC #	YARDAGE	3" STRIPS	3" SQUARES
0	1⅝ yards	17	31
1	¼ yard	2	20
2	½ yard	5	30
3	⅞ yard	9	30
4	1⅛ yards	12	30
5	1½ yards	16	30
6	⅛ yard	1	12
7	⅜ yard	4	24
8	¾ yard	8	24
9	1 yard	11	24
10	1⅜ yards	15	24

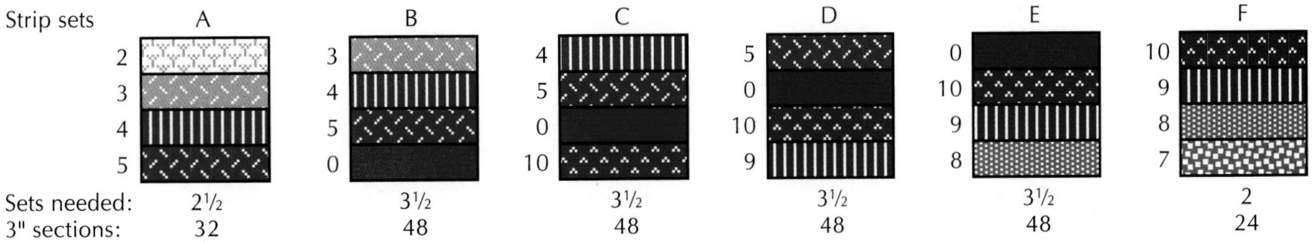

Strip sets

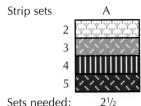

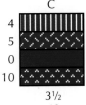
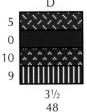
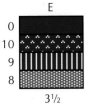
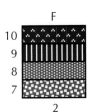

	A	B	C	D	E	F
	2	3	4	5	0	10
	3	4	5	0	10	9
	4	5	0	10	9	8
	5	0	10	9	8	7
Sets needed:	2½	3½	3½	3½	3½	2
3" sections:	32	48	48	48	48	24

Unit I—Make eight

A B C D E F E D C B A B C D E F E D C B A B C D E F E D C B A

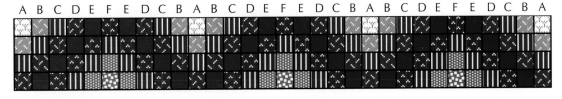

Single Square Unit II—Make five

1 2 3 4 5 0 5 4 3 2 1 2 3 4 5 0 5 4 3 2 1 2 3 4 5 0 5 4 3 2 1

Single Square Unit III—Make four

0 10 9 8 7 6 7 8 9 10 0 0 10 9 8 7 6 7 8 9 10 0 0 10 9 8 7 6 7 8 9 10 0

INSTRUCTIONS

Refer to the Many Trips Around the World basic instructions starting on page 30, if needed.

Step 1. Cut the required number of 3" strips needed from each fabric.

Step 2. Stack the strips needed for each strip set. When a half strip set is required, simply cut the full strips in half. Set aside the remaining strips to be cut later into single squares.

Step 3. Sew the required number of strip sets.

Step 4. Press the seam allowances of the strip sets in the following directions: Strip Sets A press toward Fabrics 2 and 4; Strip Sets B and C press toward Fabrics 4 and 0; Strip Sets D and E press toward Fabrics 0 and 9; and Strip Sets F press toward Fabrics 9 and 7. The seam allowances will alternate directions throughout the strip sets.

Step 5. Stack and cut the strips sets into 3" sections.

Step 6. Sew the sections together to form Unit I. Make eight of Unit I.

Step 7. Press the seam allowances of four Units I to the right and four Units I to the left.

Step 8. Using the remaining strips that were set aside in Step 2, cut the required number of 3" single squares from each fabric.

Step 9. Sew the single squares together to form Single Square Units II and III. Five of Single Square Unit II are needed and four of Single Square Units III are needed.

Step 10. Press all the seam allowances to the right.

Step 11. Lay the units together so the pressed seam allowances will nest together at the seam line. Sew the units together in the order shown.

Step 12. Refer to the instructions starting on page 10 for adding borders, if desired.

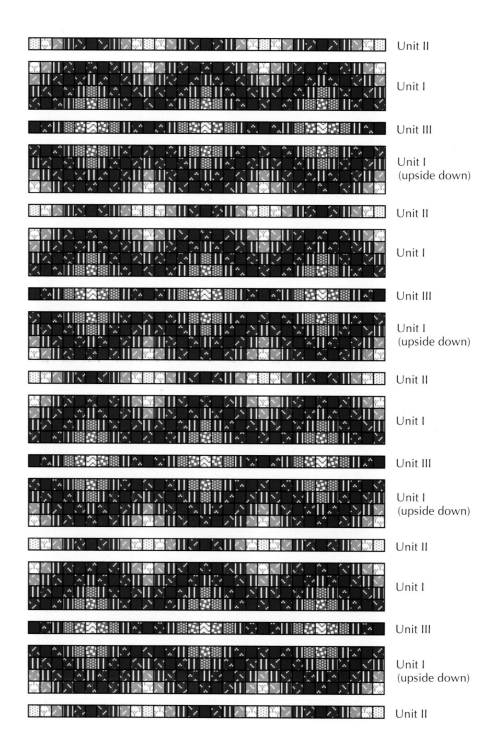

Unit II

Unit I

Unit III

Unit I
(upside down)

Unit II

Unit I

Unit III

Unit I
(upside down)

Unit II

Unit I

Unit III

Unit I
(upside down)

Unit II

Unit I

Unit III

Unit I
(upside down)

Unit II

CHAPTER 4

SUNSHINE AND SHADOW

◆

Golden Glow

SUNSHINE AND SHADOW
77½" x 92½" without borders
2½" finished square
(3" cut strips; 3" cut sections)

Fabric requirements: one yard each of eight fabrics ranging in value from Fabric 1, the lightest, to the Fabric 8, the darkest.

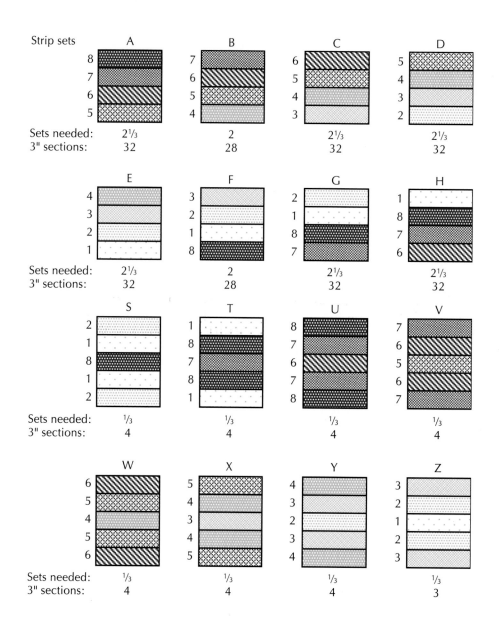

Unit I
Make four

G H A B C D E F G H A B C D E F E D C B A H G F E D C B A H G

Unit II
Make four

C D E F G H A B C D E F G H A B A H G F E D C B A H G F E D C

Unit III
Make one

S T U V W X Y Z S T U V W X Y Z Y X W V U T S Z Y X W V U T S

The Sunshine and Shadow quilt is made of nine units that span the width of the quilt. There are four each of Units I and II, and one of Unit III. The top and bottom of the quilt is formed by sewing together two each of Units I and II. These combined units are then sewn to either side of a Unit III, which makes up the center of the quilt and completes the design.

INSTRUCTIONS

Refer to the basic instructions starting on page 5, if needed.

Step 1. Cut eleven 3" strips from each fabric. From these strips, leave eight strips full length and cut the remaining three strips into thirds, or cut each of the three strips into three 14" lengths.

Step 2. Sew the required strips sets, always starting with the top strips in each set.

Step 3. Press the seam allowances of the strip sets toward the even-numbered fabrics in each strip set.

Step 4. Stack and cut the strip sets into 3" sections.

Step 5. Refer to Many Trips Around the World basic instructions starting on page 30 for stacking the cut sections, if needed. Stack the cut sections in the order they will be sewn in the units. Stack four of Unit I, four of Unit II, and one of Unit III.

Step 6. Sew the sections into units. Refer to Many Trips Around the World basic instructions starting on page 30 for sewing the units, if needed.

Step 7. Press the seams of two each of Units I and Units III toward the right. Press the seams of two each of Units I and Units II toward the left.

Step 8. Lay the units together so the pressed seam allowances will nest together at each seam line. Sew the units together in the order shown.

Step 9. Refer to the instructions starting on page 10 for adding borders, if desired.

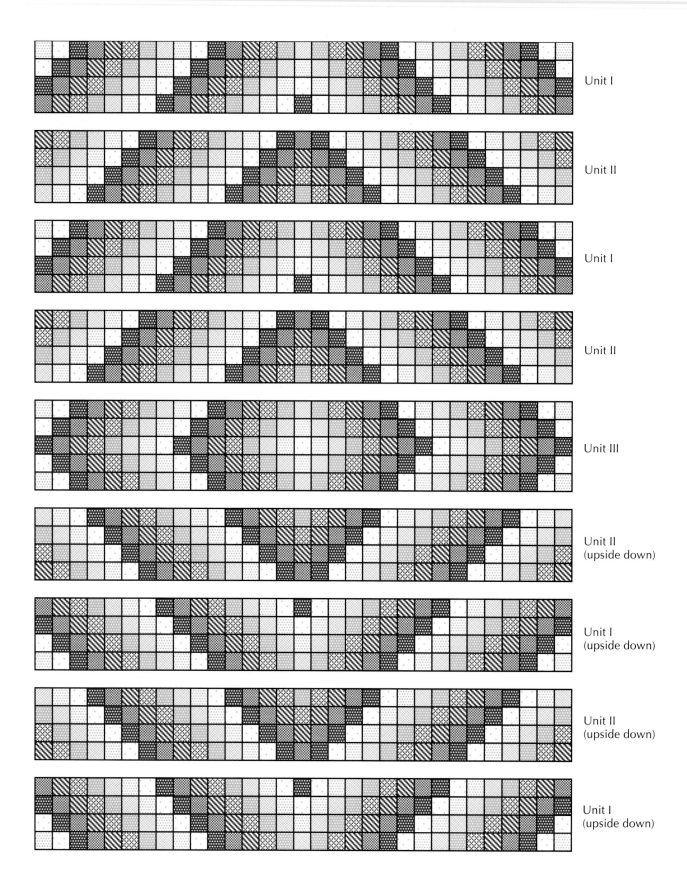

Unit I

Unit II

Unit I

Unit II

Unit III

Unit II
(upside down)

Unit I
(upside down)

Unit II
(upside down)

Unit I
(upside down)

BABY
SUNSHINE AND SHADOW

◆

Missy's Quilt

BABY SUNSHINE AND SHADOW
42" x 54" without borders
2" finished square
(2½" cut strips; 2½" cut sections)

Fabric requirements: ⅝ yard each of six fabrics ranging in value
from Fabric 1, the lightest, to Fabric 6, the darkest.

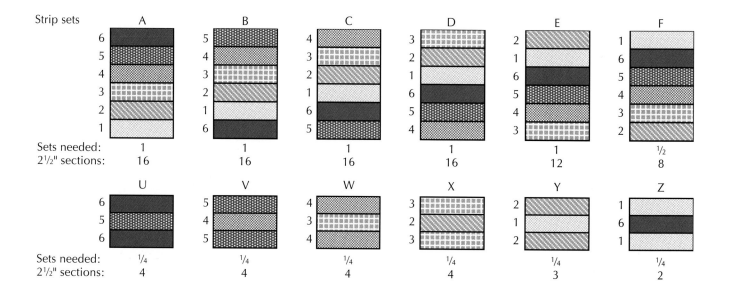

Strip sets	A	B	C	D	E	F
Sets needed:	1	1	1	1	1	½
2½" sections:	16	16	16	16	12	8

	U	V	W	X	Y	Z
Sets needed:	¼	¼	¼	¼	¼	¼
2½" sections:	4	4	4	4	3	2

Unit I
Make four

A B C D E F A B C D E D C B A F E D C B A

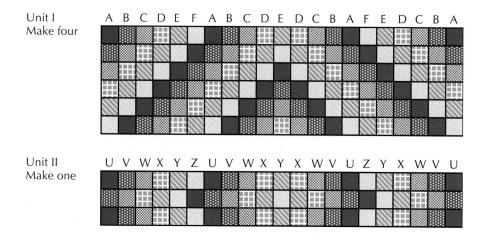

Unit II
Make one

U V W X Y Z U V W X Y X W V U Z Y X W V U

The Sunshine and Shadow baby quilt is made of five units that span the width of the quilt. There are four of Unit I and one of Unit II. Two of Unit I are joined to form the top and bottom of the quilt. These combined units are then sewn to either side of Unit II, which makes up the center of the quilt and completes the design.

INSTRUCTIONS

Refer to the basic instructions starting on page 5, if needed.

Step 1. Cut seven 2½" strips from each fabric. From these strips, leave five full length, cut one in half (for two 21" strips), and cut one into quarters (for four 10½" strips).

Step 2. Sew the required strip sets, always starting with the top strips in each set.

Step 3. Press the seams of the strip sets toward the even-numbered fabrics in each strip set.

Step 4. Stack and cut the strip sets into 2½" sections. Keep track of the top fabric in each section.

Step 5. Sew the sections into units. Make four of Unit I and one of Unit II.

Step 6. Press the seams after the sections are sewn together. Press the seams of Unit II and two of Unit I toward the left. Press the seams of the two remaining Units I toward the right.

Step 7. Lay the units together so the pressed seam allowances will nest together at each seam line. Sew the units together in the order shown.

Step 8. Refer to the instructions starting on page 10 for adding borders, if desired.

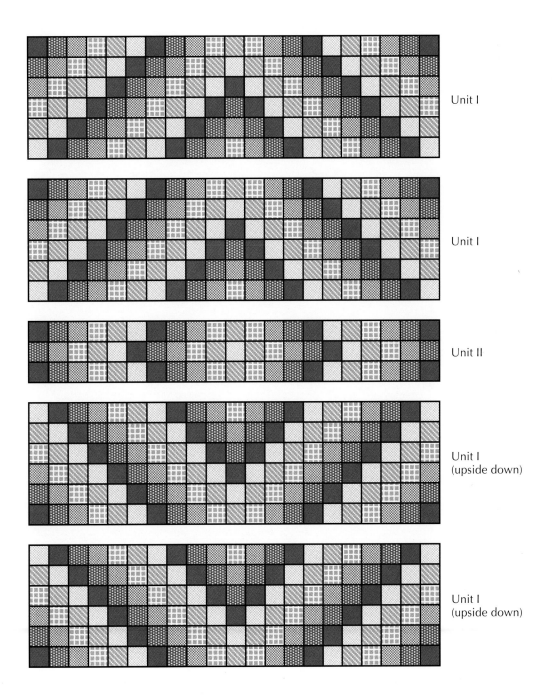

Unit I

Unit I

Unit II

Unit I
(upside down)

Unit I
(upside down)

EVENING SHADOWS

Peaceful Evening, fabrics courtesy of P&B Textiles

EVENING SHADOWS
82" x 100" without borders
4" x 2" finished rectangle
(4½" cut strips; 2½" cut sections)

Fabric requirements: 1¼ yards each of eight fabrics, ranging in color value
from Fabric 1, the lightest, to Fabric 8, the darkest.

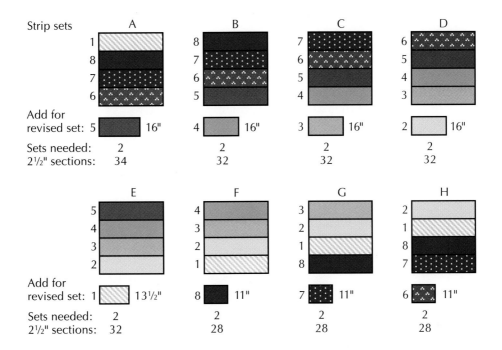

	A	B	C	D
Strip sets	1	8	7	6
	8	7	6	5
	7	6	5	4
	6	5	4	3
Add for revised set:	5 16"	4 16"	3 16"	2 16"
Sets needed:	2	2	2	2
2½" sections:	34	32	32	32

	E	F	G	H
	5	4	3	2
	4	3	2	1
	3	2	1	8
	2	1	8	7
Add for revised set:	1 13½"	8 11"	7 11"	6 11"
Sets needed:	2	2	2	2
2½" sections:	32	28	28	28

Unit I
Make three
and one revised

A B C D E F G H A B C D E F G H A B C D E D C B A H G F E D C B A H G F E D C B A

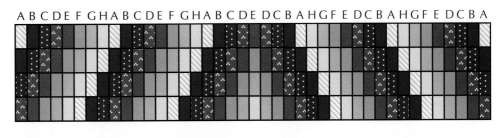

Unit II
Make two

E F G H A B C D E F G H A B C D E F G H A H G F E D C B A H G F E D C B A H G F E

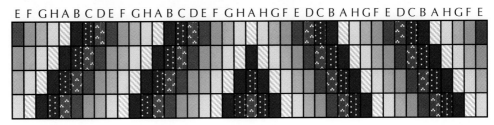

INSTRUCTIONS

Refer to the basic instructions starting on page 5, if needed.

Step 1. Cut nine 4½" wide strips of each fabric. Set aside one strip from each group.

Step 2. Sew the required strip sets. Do not cut the strip sets into sections until the strip sets are revised, as explained in the next step.

Step 3. To complete the center of the quilt design, a horizontal odd row needs to be added. This is achieved easily by revising the strip sets, or adding a partial strip to *one* of each group of strip sets. Using the 4½" wide strips (one of each fabric) that were set aside in Step 1, cut the strips to the following lengths: 13½" strip for Fabric 1, 16" strip for Fabrics 2, 3, 4 and 5, and an 11" strip for Fabrics 6, 7 and 8. These strips allow 1" for squaring up.

You now need to sew these partial strips onto the bottom edge of the designated strip sets. Of course, these partial strips will not be the same length as the strip sets. The sections cut from the revised area of these strip sets will contain five fabrics rather than four, and will be sewn together in one Unit I, which we call Revised Unit I. Add a 13½" strip of Fabric 1 to Strip Set E. Add a 16" strip of Fabric 2 to Strip Set D. Add a 16" strip of Fabric 3 to Strip Set C. Add a 16" strip of Fabric 4 to Strip Set B. Add a 16" strip of Fabric 5 to Strip Set A. Add an 11" strip of Fabric 6 to Strip Set H. Add an 11" strip of Fabric 7 to Strip Set G. Add an 11" strip of Fabric 8 to Strip Set F.

Step 4. Press the seam allowances in all of the strip sets toward the even-numbered fabrics.

Step 5. Stack and cut the strip sets into 2½" sections. Set aside the sections cut for the Revised Unit I (remember, these have five fabrics). For the Revised Unit I, you will need six each of Sections A, B, C, and D, five of Sections E, and four each of Sections F, G, and H.

Step 6. Stack the cut sections in the order they will be sewn into units. Stack piles for three of Unit I, one of Revised Unit I, and two of Unit II.

Step 7. Sew the sections into units.

Step 8. Press the seams of the three Units I and the Revised Unit I toward the left. Press the seams of the two Units II toward the right.

Step 9. The pressed seams will nest together at each seam line. Sew the units together in the order shown. Note that in the bottom half of the quilt the units are turned upside down to mirror the design in the top half. The row of fabrics added to the Revised Unit I is the horizontal center of the quilt top.

Step 10. Refer to the instructions starting on page 10 for adding borders, if desired.

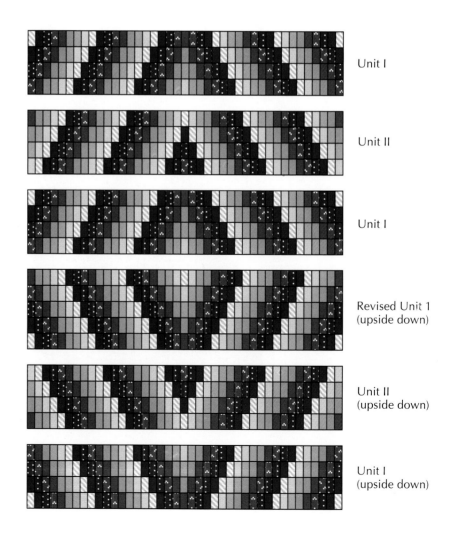

Unit I

Unit II

Unit I

Revised Unit 1 (upside down)

Unit II (upside down)

Unit I (upside down)

Navajo

NAVAJO
78¾" x 101¼" without borders
3¾" x 1¾" finished rectangle
(4¼" cut strips; 2¼" cut sections)

The construction of the Navajo quilt begins with cutting and sewing 4¼" wide strips into strip sets. These strip sets are cut into sections at 2¼" increments. The three different units that span the width of the quilt top are formed by sewing the sections together. There are four of Unit I, two of Unit II, and one of Unit III. The four Units I are sewn on either side of the two Units II to form the top and bottom of the quilt. These two large sections are then sewn on either side of Unit III to complete the design of the quilt. (For a slightly larger quilt, which finishes 90" x 108" without borders, cut the strips at 4½" increments and the sections at 2½" increments. The yardage and strip requirements remain the same.)

FABRIC #	YARDAGE	4¼" STRIPS
1	1½ yards	11
2	1½ yards	11
3	1½ yards	11
4	1⅜ yards	10
5	1⅜ yards	10
6	1⅜ yards	10
7	1⅜ yards	10
8	1⅜ yards	10

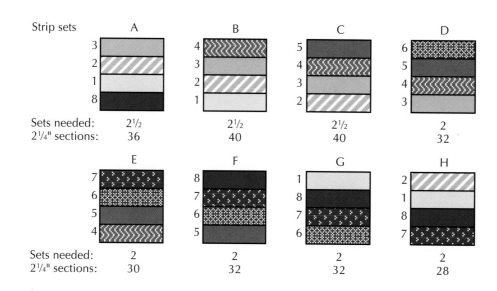

Strip sets	A	B	C	D
	3	4	5	6
	2	3	4	5
	1	2	3	4
	8	1	2	3
Sets needed:	2½	2½	2½	2
2¼" sections:	36	40	40	32

	E	F	G	H
	7	8	1	2
	6	7	8	1
	5	6	7	8
	4	5	6	7
Sets needed:	2	2	2	2
2¼" sections:	30	32	32	28

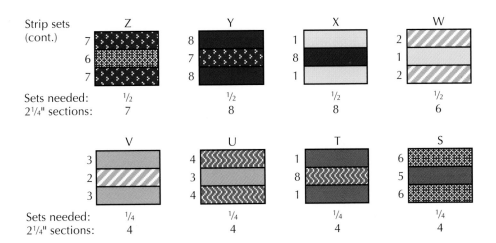

Strip sets (cont.)	Z	Y	X	W
	7	8	1	2
	6	7	8	1
	7	8	1	2
Sets needed:	1/2	1/2	1/2	1/2
2¼" sections:	7	8	8	6

	V	U	T	S
	3	4	1	6
	2	3	8	5
	3	4	1	6
Sets needed:	1/4	1/4	1/4	1/4
2¼" sections:	4	4	4	4

INSTRUCTIONS

Refer to the basic instructions starting on page 5, if needed.

Step 1. Cut the needed number of 4¼" strips from each of the eight fabrics.

Step 2. Sew the strips together to make the required number of each strip set. For strip sets that require half a strip set, simply cut the strips in half (these should be at least 21" long). For those strip sets requiring a quarter strip set, cut a half strip in half again (these should be at least 10½" long). Cut the strips to the necessary length before sewing the strip sets.

Step 3. Press the seam allowances of the strip sets toward the even-numbered fabrics in each strip set.

Step 4. Review the basic instructions starting on page 9 for stacking and cutting the strip sets, if needed. Cut the strip sets into 2¼" sections.

Step 5. Stack the sections in the order they will be sewn into units. Stack four of Unit I, two of Unit II, and one of Unit III.

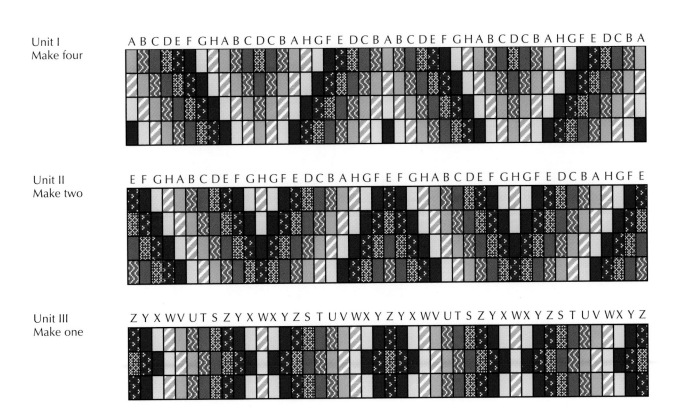

Unit I
Make four

A B C D E F G H A B C D C B A H G F E D C B A B C D E F G H A B C D C B A H G F E D C B A

Unit II
Make two

E F G H A B C D E F G H G F E D C B A H G F E F G H A B C D E F G H G F E D C B A H G F E

Unit III
Make one

Z Y X W V U T S Z Y X W X Y Z S T U V W X Y Z Y X W V U T S Z Y X W X Y Z S T U V W X Y Z

Step 6. Sew the sections together to make four of Unit I, two of Unit II, and one of Unit III. Notice that the seams have been pressed so they alternate at each intersection. Be sure to align the seam lines.

Step 7. Press the seams of two Units I, one Unit II, and Unit III toward the left. Press the seams of two Units I and one Unit II toward the right.

Step 8. Lay the units together so the pressed seams will nest together at each seam line. Sew the units together in the order shown. Note that in the bottom half of the quilt the units are turned upside down to mirror the design in the top half. Unit III is the horizontal center of the quilt top.

Step 9. Refer to the instructions starting on page 10 for adding borders, if desired.

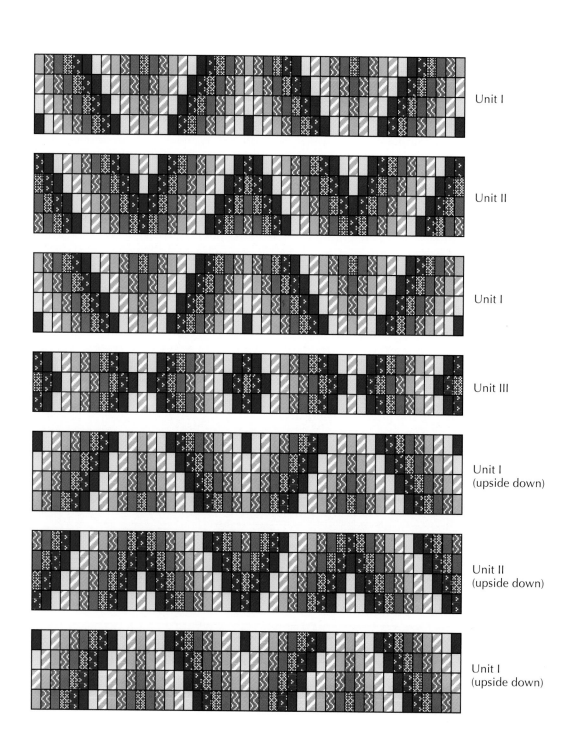

Unit I

Unit II

Unit I

Unit III

Unit I
(upside down)

Unit II
(upside down)

Unit I
(upside down)

ZUNI

Zuni

ZUNI
86¼" x 106¾" without borders
1¾" x 3¾" finished rectangle
(2¼" cut strips; 4¼" cut sections)

Fabric requirements: 1¼ yards each of ten fabrics

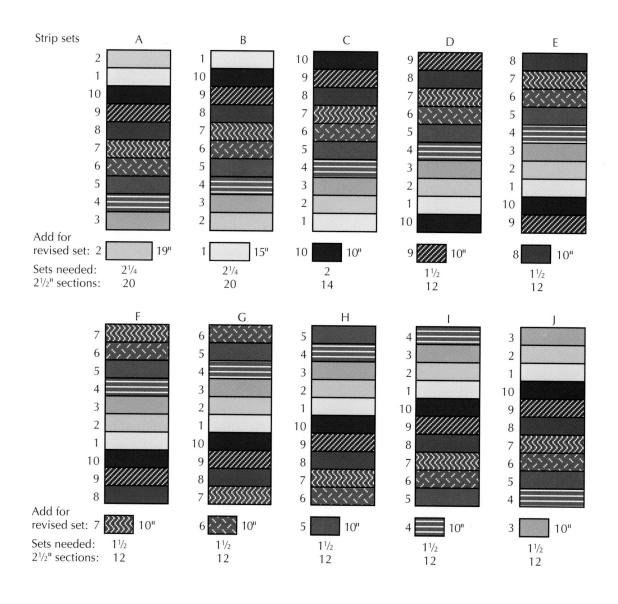

Strip sets

	A	B	C	D	E
	2	1	10	9	8
	1	10	9	8	7
	10	9	8	7	6
	9	8	7	6	5
	8	7	6	5	4
	7	6	5	4	3
	6	5	4	3	2
	5	4	3	2	1
	4	3	2	1	10
	3	2	1	10	9

Add for
revised set: 2   19"   1   15"   10   10"   9   10"   8   10"

| Sets needed: | 2¼ | 2¼ | 2 | 1½ | 1½ |
| 2½" sections: | 20 | 20 | 14 | 12 | 12 |

	F	G	H	I	J
	7	6	5	4	3
	6	5	4	3	2
	5	4	3	2	1
	4	3	2	1	10
	3	2	1	10	9
	2	1	10	9	8
	1	10	9	8	7
	10	9	8	7	6
	9	8	7	6	5
	8	7	6	5	4

Add for
revised set: 7   10"   6   10"   5   10"   4   10"   3   10"

| Sets needed: | 1½ | 1½ | 1½ | 1½ | 1½ |
| 2½" sections: | 12 | 12 | 12 | 12 | 12 |

Unit I
Make three and one revised

A B C D E F G H I J A B A J I H G F E D C B A

Unit II
Make two

B C D E F G H I J A B C B A J I H G F E D C B

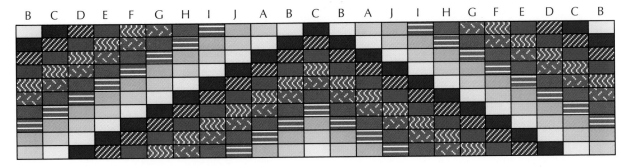

INSTRUCTIONS

Refer to the basic instructions starting on page 5, if needed.

Step 1. Cut eighteen 2¼" strips from each fabric. From these strips, cut four strips in half and cut one of these half strips in half again. You should have fifteen full strips, seven half strips, and two quarter strips.

Step 2. Stack the strips needed for each strip set. You will have one full strip of each fabric remaining, which will be used in the revised strip sets explained in Step 4.

Step 3. Sew the required strip sets, always starting with the top strips in each set.

Step 4. To complete the center of the quilt design, a horizontal odd row needs to be added. This is achieved easily by revising the strip sets, or adding a partial strip to one of each group of strip sets. The sections cut from these revised strips will be sewn together in what we call the Revised Unit I. Using the strips remaining in Step 2, cut the strips to the following lengths: 15" strip for Fabric 1, 19" for Fabric 2, and 10" strips for Fabrics 3 through 10.

You now need to sew these partial strips onto the bottom of the designated strip sets as follows: Fabric 1 (15" strip) to the bottom of the full Strip Set B, Fabric 2 (19" strip) to the bottom of the full Strip Set A, Fabric 3 (10" strip) to the bottom of the half Strip Set J, Fabric 4 (10" strip) to the bottom of the half Strip Set I, Fabric 5 (10" strip) to the bottom of the half Strip Set H, Fabric 6 (10" strip) to the bottom of the half Strip Set G, Fabric 7 (10" strip) to the bottom of the half Strip Set F, Fabric 8 (10" strip) to the bottom of the half Strip Set E, Fabric 9 (10" strip) to the bottom of the half Strip Set D, and Fabric 10 (10" strip) to the bottom of a full Strip Set C.

Step 5. Press the seam allowances toward the even-numbered fabrics in each strip set.

Step 6. Cut the strip sets into 4¼" sections. As you cut the sections for the Revised Unit I, set them aside in their own pile. You will need four sections of Revised Strip Set A, three sections of Revised Strip Set B, and two sections of Revised Strip Sets C, D, E, F, G, H, I, and J.

Step 7. Stack the cut sections in the order they will be sewn into the units. Stack three of Unit I, one of Revised Unit I, and two of Unit II.

Step 8. Sew the sections into units.

Step 9. Press the seam allowances of all the units to the left.

Step 10. At this time, it is helpful to lay the units on a large table or floor in the order they will be sewn, as shown. Note that the row of fabrics added to Revised Unit I is the horizontal center of the quilt. The seams have been pressed to nest together at each seam line. Sew the units together in the order shown.

Step 11. Refer to the instructions starting on page 10 for adding borders, if desired.

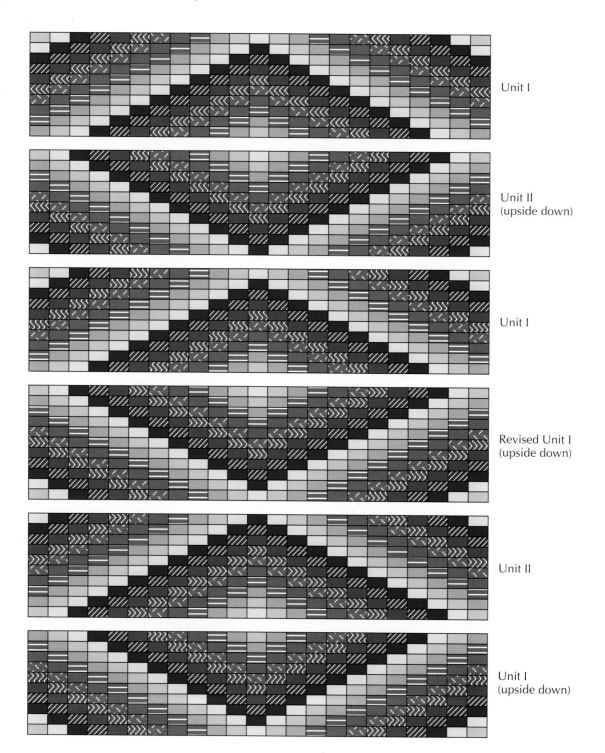

Unit I

Unit II (upside down)

Unit I

Revised Unit I (upside down)

Unit II

Unit I (upside down)

ZULU

Zulu

ZULU

78¾" x 96¼" without borders
1¾" x 3½" finished rectangles
(2¼" cut strips; 4¼" cut sections)

Fabric requirements: 1⅛ yards each of nine fabrics.

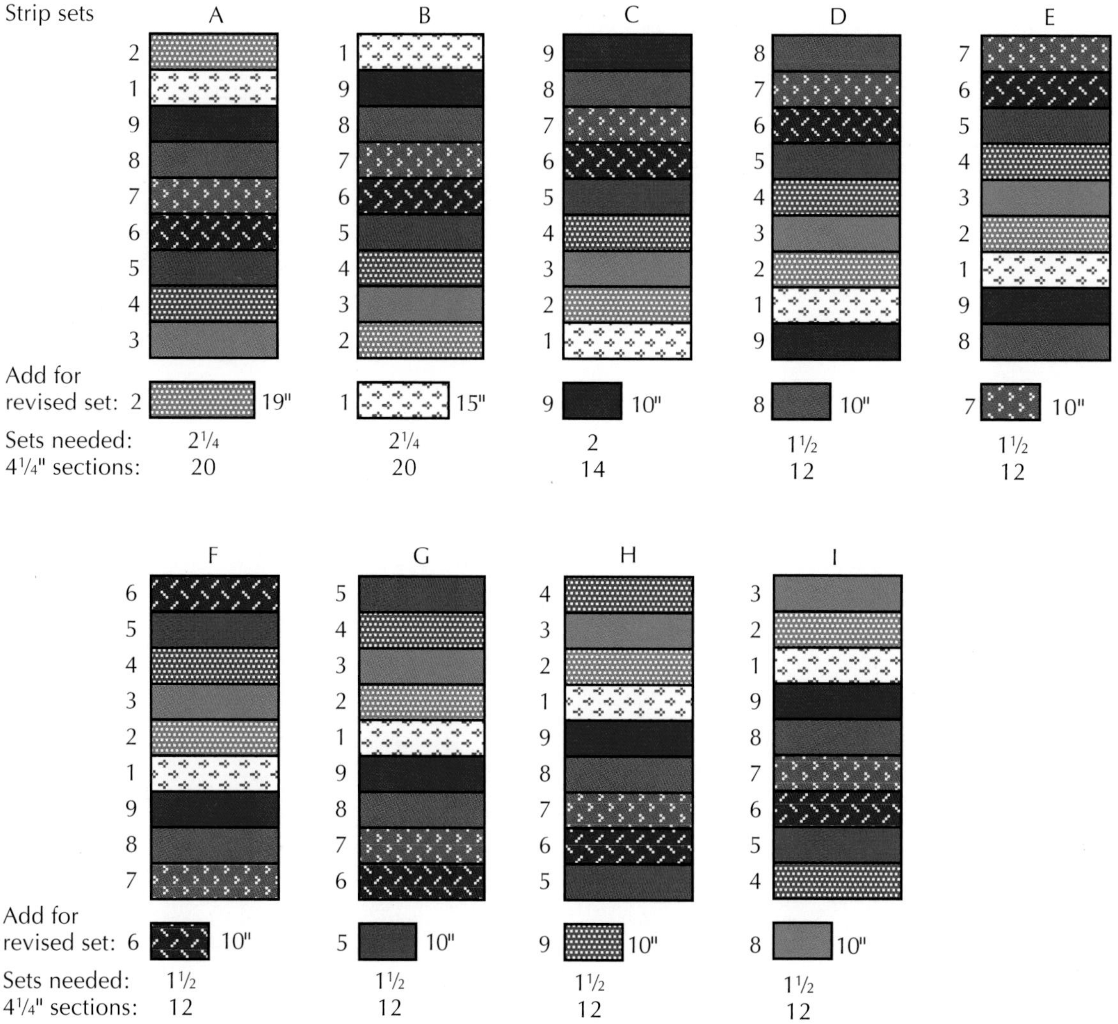
Strip sets
A: 2, 1, 9, 8, 7, 6, 5, 4, 3
Add for revised set: 2 19"
Sets needed: 2¼
4¼" sections: 20
B: 1, 9, 8, 7, 6, 5, 4, 3, 2
1 15"
2¼
20
C: 9, 8, 7, 6, 5, 4, 3, 2, 1
9 10"
2
14
D: 8, 7, 6, 5, 4, 3, 2, 1, 9
8 10"
1½
12
E: 7, 6, 5, 4, 3, 2, 1, 9, 8
7 10"
1½
12
F: 6, 5, 4, 3, 2, 1, 9, 8, 7
Add for revised set: 6 10"
Sets needed: 1½
4¼" sections: 12
G: 5, 4, 3, 2, 1, 9, 8, 7, 6
5 10"
1½
12
H: 4, 3, 2, 1, 9, 8, 7, 6, 5
9 10"
1½
12
I: 3, 2, 1, 9, 8, 7, 6, 5, 4
8 10"
1½
12

Unit I
Make three and one revised

A B C D E F G H I A B A I H G F E D C B A

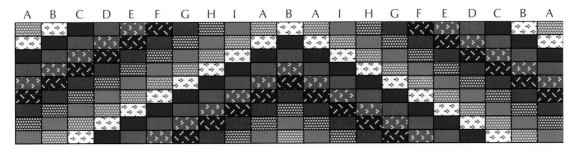

Unit II
Make two

B C D E F G H I A B C B A I H G F E D C B

INSTRUCTIONS

Review the basic instructions starting on page 5, if needed.

Step 1. Cut sixteen 2¼" strips from each fabric. From these strips, cut four strips in half and cut one of these half strips in half again. You should have 12 full strips, seven half strips, and two quarter strips.

Step 2. Stack the strips needed for each strip set. You will have one half strip of each fabric remaining, which will be used in the revised strip sets explained in Step 4.

Step 3. Sew the required strip sets, always starting with the top strips in each set.

Step 4. To complete the center of the quilt design, a horizontal odd row needs to be added. This is achieved easily by revising the strip sets, or adding a partial strip to one of each group of strip sets. The sections cut from these revised strips will be sewn together in what we call Revised Unit I. Using the strip sets remaining in Step 2, cut the strips to the following lengths: 15" for Fabric 1, 19" strip for Fabric 2, 10" strips for Fabrics 3 through 9.

You now need to sew these partial strips to the bottom of the designated strip sets as follows: Fabric 1 (15" strip) to the bottom of a full Strip Set B,

Fabric 2 (19" strip) to the bottom of a full Strip Set A, Fabric 3 (10" strip) to the bottom of the half Strip Set I, Fabric 4 (10" strip) to the bottom of the half Strip Set H, Fabric 5 (10" strip) to the bottom of the half Strip Set G, Fabric 6 (10" strip) to the bottom of the half Strip Set F, Fabric 7 (10" strip) to the bottom of the half Strip Set E, Fabric 8 (10" strip) to the bottom of the half Strip Set D, Fabric 9 (10" strip) to the bottom of a full Strip Set C.

Step 5. Press the seam allowances of the strip sets as follows: For Strip Sets A, B, and C, press first in one direction and then in the other. This will allow you to flip the seam allowances to the direction needed. For Strip Sets D, F, and H, press toward the top strip. Press the seams in Strip Sets E, G, and I toward the bottom strip.

Step 6. Cut the strip sets into 4¼" sections. As you cut the sections for the Revised Unit I, set them aside in their own pile. You will need four sections of Revised Strip Set A, three sections of Revised Strip Set B, and two sections of Revised Strip Sets C, D, E, F, G, H, and I.

Step 7. Stack the cut sections in the order they will be sewn into the units. Stack three of Unit I, one of Revised Unit I, and two of Unit II.

Step 8. Sew the sections into units.

Step 9. Press the seam allowances of all the units to the left.

Step 10. At this time, it is helpful to lay the units on a large table or floor in the order they will be sewn, as shown. Note that the row of fabrics added to Revised Unit I is the horizontal center of the quilt top. The pressed seams will nest together at each seam line. Sew the units together in the order shown.

Step 11. Refer to the instructions starting on page 10 for adding borders, if desired.

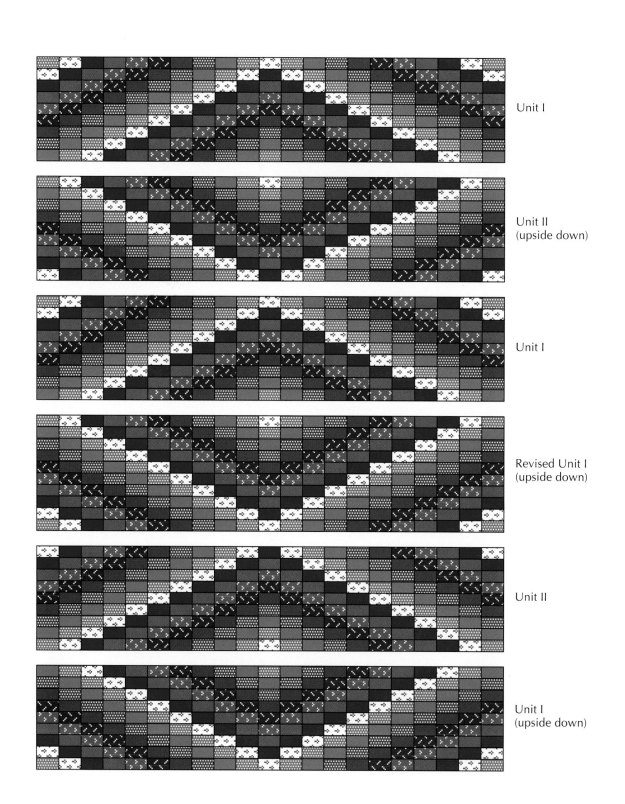

Unit I

Unit II
(upside down)

Unit I

Revised Unit I
(upside down)

Unit II

Unit I
(upside down)

CHAPTER 5

NINE PATCH AND IRISH CHAIN
BASIC SEWING INSTRUCTIONS

◆

Nine Patch blocks are just what the name implies: nine squares sewn together. If you look at a Nine Patch block, you will see that the blocks are also three columns of three squares sewn together. These columns of three squares can be cut from strip sets of three strips sewn together. The strip sets facilitate the construction of the Nine Patch block, resulting in an accurate and square Nine Patch block.

SEWING THE NINE PATCH

Refer to the basic instructions starting on page 8 for sewing, pressing, stacking, and cutting the strip sets.

Step 1. To sew the columns into blocks, begin with a column or section of the first strip set that's laying face up. Lay a section from the second strip set face down on the first, lining up the seam lines. Notice that the seam allowances are pressed in opposing directions. Using your fingertips, feel if the seams butt up against one another. There should not be a gap or space between the seams. Sew consistently with a scant ¼" seam allowance. Chain piece the two column sections together. Add the third column face down on the second.

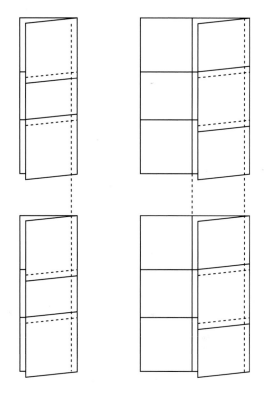

Step 2. Press the seam allowances toward the outside columns. Consider these last seams as the vertical seams of the Nine Patch blocks.

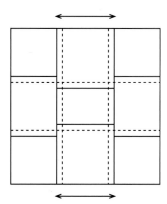

Pressing the completed Nine Patch

BLOOMING NINE PATCH

Carribean Cove

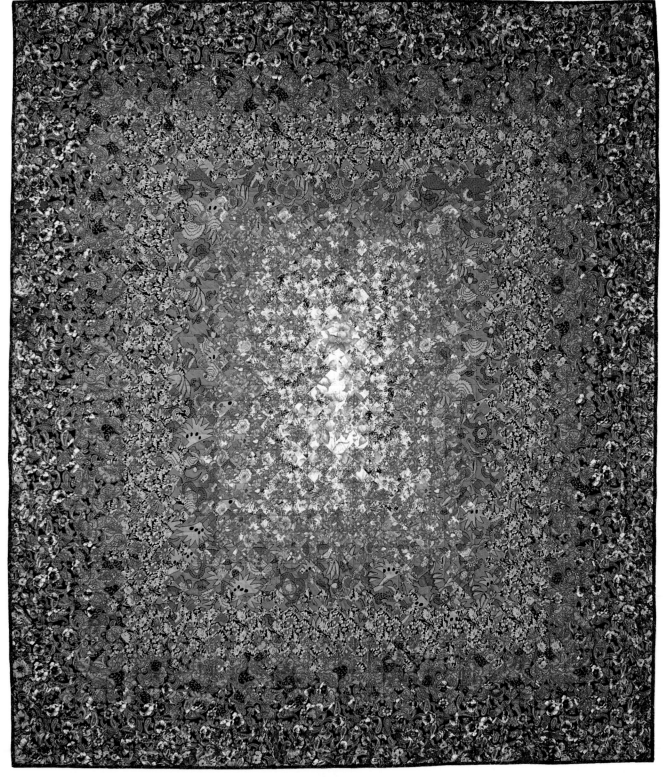

Colorburst

BLOOMING NINE PATCH
72" x 82" without borders
3¾" finished square

Although this quilt design looks very complicated, it is actually very simple to make. It is constructed of alternating Nine Patches and plain squares. The design starts in the center of the quilt with three plain squares of the first fabric set on the diagonal. The next row, or course, consists of Nine Patches made of the first and second fabrics that are placed around the first three squares. The following course is plain squares of the second fabric, and then a course of Nine Patches made of the second and third fabrics. This creates a look of the fabrics changing without actually being able to see the seams, or blocks, which create the change.

The fabric selection is the most important part of this quilt—large flowery or busy prints are perfect for this project. A color theme is not necessary, but can be implemented. The color values of the fabrics create the change. The *Colorburst* quilt on page 79

changes colors throughout the quilt; it starts with yellow and green, and ends with pink and purple. The basic idea behind this quilt is that each fabric shares one or two colors of the preceding fabric to help the fabrics blend together and create the "bloom." For example, the *Colorburst* quilt begins with a fabric with a white background and yellow, blue, pink and green flowers, while the second fabric is a yellow, green, pink, red, and purple floral. These first two fabrics have yellow, green and pink in common. The third fabric is purple, pink, red, orange, and teal. The shared colors in Fabrics 2 and 3 are purple, pink, and teal. Fabric 4 is teal, orange, red, green, yellow, and blue—sharing teal, orange, and red with Fabric 3. This "color sharing" continues through to Fabric 8 and the last course around the quilt are triangles of Fabric 8.

FABRIC #	YARDAGE
1	⅜ yard
2	⅝ yard
3	¾ yard
4	1 yard
5	1⅜ yards
6	1⅝ yards
7	1⅞ yards
8	1⅛ yards

Number of strips to cut

FABRIC #	1¾" STRIPS	4¼" STRIPS	6⅝" STRIPS
1	3	1	
2	6	2	
3	9	2	
4	12	3	
5	15	4	
6	18	5	
7	21	6	
8	10	-	3

INSTRUCTIONS

Refer to the basic instructions starting on page 5, if needed.

Step 1. Cut the required number of 1¾" strips from each fabric.

Step 2. Stack the strips needed for each strip set. If a half strip set is required, simply cut the full strips in half. Sew the required number of strip sets.

Step 3. Stack the strip sets face down in staggered piles, and cut 1¾" sections. Review the instructions on page 77 to construct the Nine Patch blocks.

Step 4. Press the seam allowances of the outside column strip sets toward the outer strips. Press the seam allowance of the center column strip sets toward the center strips.

Step 5. Sew the required number of each group of Nine Patch blocks.

Step 6. Press the seam allowances toward the outside columns. Consider these last seams as vertical seams when sewing the rows together later.

Step 7. Cut the required number of 4¼" strips from each fabric. Lay the strips horizontally (the cross grain of the fabric will be likewise). Cut these strips

Total nine patches		Outside column		Sets needed	1¾" sections	Center column		Sets needed	1¾" sections
8	A	A	1 / 2 / 1	1	16	A	2 / 1 / 2	½	8
16	B	B	2 / 3 / 2	1½	32	B	3 / 2 / 3	1	16
24	C	C	3 / 4 / 3	2	48	C	4 / 3 / 4	1	24
32	D	D	4 / 5 / 4	3	64	D	5 / 4 / 5	1½	32
40	E	E	5 / 6 / 5	3½	80	E	6 / 5 / 6	2	40
48	F	F	6 / 7 / 6	4	96	F	7 / 6 / 7	2	48
56	G	G	7 / 8 / 7	5	112	G	8 / 7 / 8	2½	56

into 4 ¼" squares. As the squares are cut, place them in a pile without turning them—this will keep the crosswise grain of all the squares in the same direction. (Refer to single square units on page 30 of the Many Trips Around the World basic instructions). Check the chart for the number of plain squares needed of each fabric. Note that there are no plain squares cut from Fabric 8 since these are triangles cut from a larger square.

FABRIC #	PLAIN SQUARES	SIDE TRANGLES	CORNER TRIANGLES
1	3		
2	12		
3	20		
4	28		
5	36		
6	44		
7	52		
8	-	56	4

Step 8. The triangles used to finish the last row are cut from a 6⅝" square, which is cut twice diagonally to yield four triangles. This leaves the straight of grain on the outside of the quilt to prevent stretching. Fourteen 6⅝" triangles will yield the needed 56 triangles. Cut three 6⅝" strips of Fabric 8. Then cut the strips into fourteen 6⅝" squares without lifting the squares, and then cut them twice diagonally.

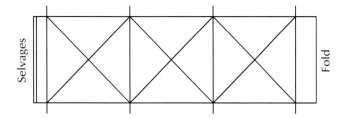

Step 9. The triangles for the four corners of the quilt are cut from two 3" squares, each cut once diagonally. These squares can be cut from the remaining fabric after cutting the larger squares in the last step.

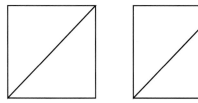

Step 10. Since the crosswise grain of fabric can stretch a little, it is very helpful to have the crosswise grain of the plain squares across the width of the row. This will allow you to ease the corners together for a perfect match. After the squares are cut, if you are unsure of the crosswise grain, take one square and hold it between your thumb and index finger of both hands and gently tug. The lengthwise grain is taut with no give and the crosswise grain will stretch a little. When sewing the rows together, always keep the crosswise grain of the plain blocks horizontal, and the vertical seams of the Nine Patches vertical. You will be sewing along the lengthwise grain of the fabric when joining the blocks.

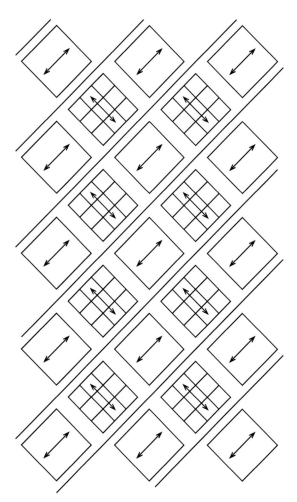

Layout of the crosswise grain of plain squares and vertical seams of Nine Patch blocks

Step 11. Now that all the Nine Patch blocks, squares, and triangles are complete, it is best if you can lay the blocks out on a floor in the order they will be in the quilt. Choose the center of a large floor, and lay the three plain squares on the diagonal. Place the eight Nine Patches A around the plain squares, as shown. Add the plain squares of Fabric 2, then the Nine Patches B. Continue alternating plain blocks and Nine Patches until you place Nine Patch G. Then place the side triangles and corner triangles, as shown.

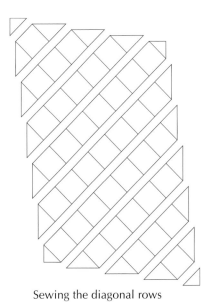

Sewing the diagonal rows

Step 12. Piece together the blocks in each diagonal row. Keep the crosswise grain of the plain squares horizontal in the rows and the vertical seams of the Nine Patches vertical (or perpendicular) in the rows. Press the seams toward the plain blocks. Once the rows are sewn and pressed, place the rows back on the floor in their order of placement in the quilt.

Step 13. To join the diagonal rows together, we recommend starting with one of the long center rows and adding rows as you work out toward the corner, until you have made one diagonal "half" of the quilt top. Then start with another long center row (next to where you started before) and work out to the other corner. Join the two diagonal halves together. Press the seams in alternating directions.

DIAMONDBACK SCRAP

Diamondback

DIAMONDBACK SCRAP
3¾" finished square

Diamondback Scrap quilt is made from vertical rows of Nine Patch blocks and triangles. The Nine Patch blocks are set on point with triangles sewn on both sides. You can use many color themes for this quilt style. For example, the sample quilt has purples and lavenders with contrasting oranges, yellows, and rusts in both light and dark shades.

Light and dark blue shades is another favorite color theme, with accents of pink, peach, purples, and teals. Or you can just use some scrap fabrics with light and dark shades of whatever you have on hand. Yardage requirements are also provided for a planned variation using one dark, one medium, and one light fabric.

LARGE DIAMONDBACK SCRAP
73½" x 94½" without borders

Fabric requirements for Nine Patch: 1¾" strips of 24 light assorted fabrics or ⅛ yard of 12 fabrics (or 1¼ yards); 1¾" strips of 39 medium assorted fabrics or ⅛ yard of 20 fabrics (or 2 yards); 1¾" strips of 24 dark assorted fabrics or ⅛ yard of 12 fabrics (or 1¼ yard)

Fabric requirements for triangles: 3¼" strips of 23 light assorted fabrics or ¼ yard of 12 fabrics (or 2¼ yards); 3¼" strips of 23 medium assorted fabrics or ¼ yard of 12 fabrics (or 2¼ yards); 3¼" strips and 2 dark 3½" squares of six dark assorted fabrics or ⅛ yard of seven fabrics (or ¾ yard)

SMALL DIAMONDBACK SCRAP
63" x 84" without borders

Fabric requirements for Nine Patches: 1¾" strips of 18 light assorted fabrics or ⅛ yard of nine fabrics (or 1 yard); 1¾" strips of 30 medium assorted fabrics or ⅛ yard of 15 fabrics (or 1⅝ yard); 1¾" strips of 18 dark assorted fabrics or ⅛ yard of nine fabrics (or 1 yard)

Fabric requirements for triangles: 3¼" strips of 18 light assorted fabrics or ¼ yard of nine fabrics (or 1¾ yards); 3¼" strips of 18 medium assorted fabrics or ¼ yard of nine fabrics (or 1¾ yards); 3¼" strips of five dark assorted fabrics and two dark 3½" squares or ⅛ yard of six fabrics (or ⅝ yard)

		Large	Small
Strip set A			
Light			
Medium			
Dark			
Outside columns	Sets needed:	19	14
	1¾" sections cut:	442	330
Strip set B			
Medium			
Dark			
Medium			
Dark center columns	Sets needed:	5	4
	1¾" sections cut:	119	90
Strip set C			
Meduim			
Light			
Medium			
Light center columns	Sets needed:	5	4
	1¾" sections cut:	102	75
Dark Nine Patch			
A B A	Blocks needed:	119	90
Light Nine Patch			
A C A	Blocks needed:	102	75
Triangles	Light:	252	192
	Medium:	252	192
	Dark:	60	52
Nine Patches in each row	Total:	17	15
Light Nine Patches and medium triangles	Rows needed:	6	5
Dark Nine Patches and light triangles	Rows needed:	7	6

INSTRUCTIONS

Refer to the basic instructions starting on page 5, if needed.

Step 1. Cut the required number of 1¾" strips from each of the light, medium, and dark Nine Patch fabrics.

Step 2. Stack the strips needed for each strip set. Sew the required number of strip sets.

Step 3. Press the seam allowances of the strip sets: Press Strip Set A toward the outer strips, and Strip Sets B and C toward the center strips.

Step 4. Stack the strip sets face down in staggered piles, and cut 1¾" sections. Review the instructions on page 77 to construct the Nine Patch blocks.

Step 5. Sew the dark Nine Patches together. Beginning with a section from Strip Set A, face up, turn the section so the dark fabric is at the top. Lay a section from Strip Set B on top of A. Stitch the pieces together, lining up the seam lines. Add a section from Strip Set A with the dark fabric at the bottom. Stitch together. Notice how the dark fabrics are in a diagonal line through the Nine Patch. Press these seams toward the outside columns (Section A). Sew the required number of dark Nine Patches needed. Refer to the chart, if needed.

Step 6. Sew the light Nine Patches together. Beginning with a section from Strip Set A, face up, turn the section so the light fabric is at the top. Add a section from Strip Set B. Stitch the pieces together, lining up the seam lines. Add a section from Strip Set A with the light fabric at the bottom. Stitch together. Press these seams toward the outside columns. Note the light fabrics in the diagonal line. Sew the required number of light Nine Patches needed. Refer to the chart, if needed.

Step 7. Cut the necessary 3¼" strips from the light, medium, and dark fabrics for the triangles.

Step 8. Cut the amount of triangles needed using the template on page 88. Trace the template onto graph paper. Use a glue stick or rubber cement to glue the template to poster board or template plastic. Cut out the template with a paper scissors. Lay one of the 3¼" strips, folded in half, on your mat. Lay the template on the end of the strip nearest the selvages, aligning the long edge of the template with the bottom edge of the strip. Cut along the short edges of the template. Turn the template upside down and align the long edge of the template with the top edge of the fabric and the angle cut now on the end of the strip. Cut the one short edge. Continue cutting the triangles toward the fold of the strip. Unfold the remainder of the strip and cut one more triangle. Each strip will yield 11 triangles.

Step 9. Chain stitch the triangles to the Nine Patches. Always have the 90° corner of the triangle covering one of the darkest or lightest squares of the Nine Patch, as shown in the illustration. Add the triangles to one side of the Nine Patches and then to the other side. Press these seams toward the triangles.

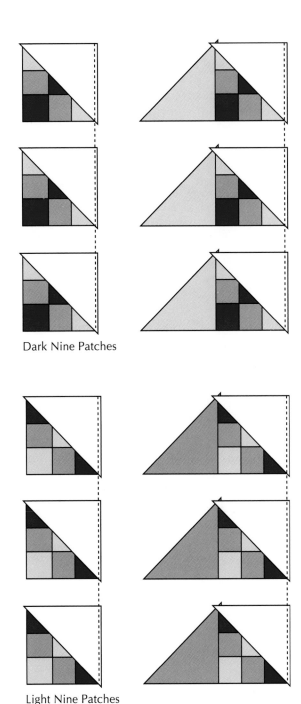

Dark Nine Patches

Light Nine Patches

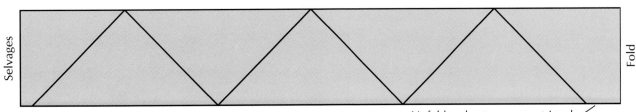

Selvages

Fold

Unfold and cut one more triangle

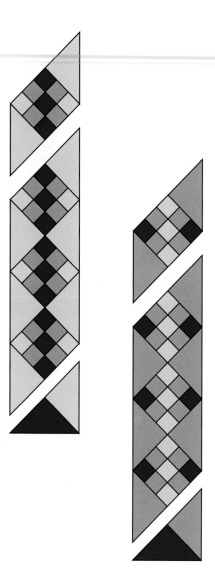

Step 10. Stitch together the number of rows needed of the dark Nine Patches with the light triangles. Finish the top and bottom of each row with one dark and one light triangle, positioning the dark triangles on the ends.

Step 11. Stitch together the number of rows needed of the light Nine Patches with the medium triangles. Finish the top and bottom of each row with one dark and one medium triangle, positioning the dark triangles on the ends.

Step 12. Sew the finished rows together, side by side, beginning with the dark Nine Patches with the light triangle row and alternating with the light Nine Patches with the medium triangle rows. You will end with a dark Nine Patch row.

Step 13. A row of medium and dark triangles need to be added to both sides of the quilt top. For the small bed quilt, sew two sets of 16 medium and 15 dark triangles as shown. For the large bed quilt, sew two sets of 18 medium and 17 dark triangles. For each size quilt, cut two dark 3½" squares, and cut these squares once diagonally to make the four corner triangles to complete each end of the side rows. Begin with the small dark corner triangle and add a medium value triangle, and then a large dark triangle. Continue alternating triangles until you have added the required number of dark and medium value triangles—you will end with a medium triangle. Add the small dark corner triangle to finish the row. Make two side rows.

Step 14. Add the side rows to each side of the quilt with the medium value triangles next to the quilt, and the dark triangles on the outside edge of the quilt.

Diamondback Triangle Template Pattern
(includes ¼" seam allowance)

Step 13

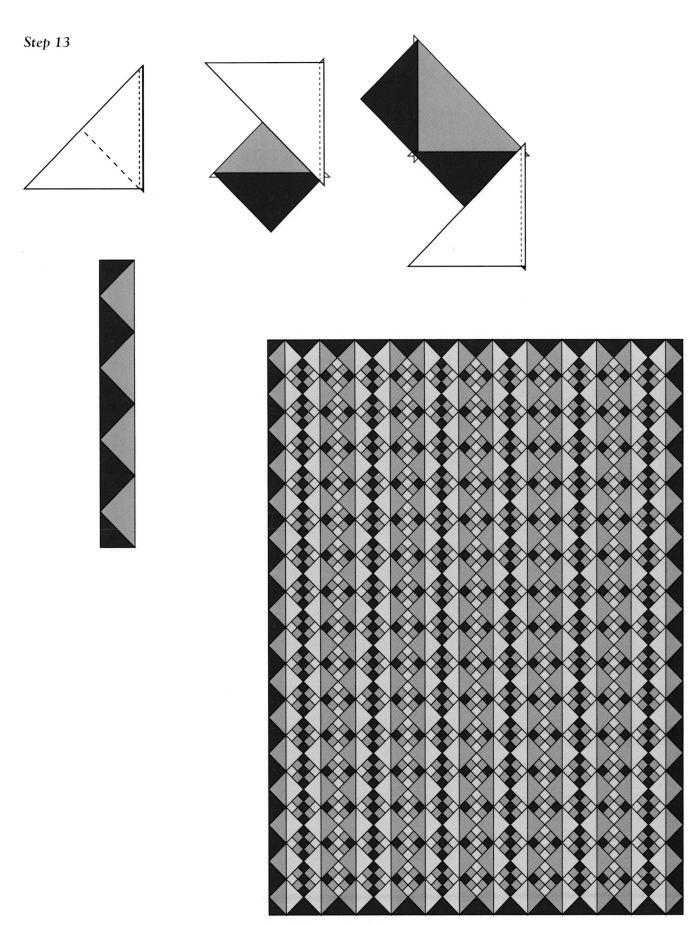

Small Diamondback Scrap

Uneven Nine Patch

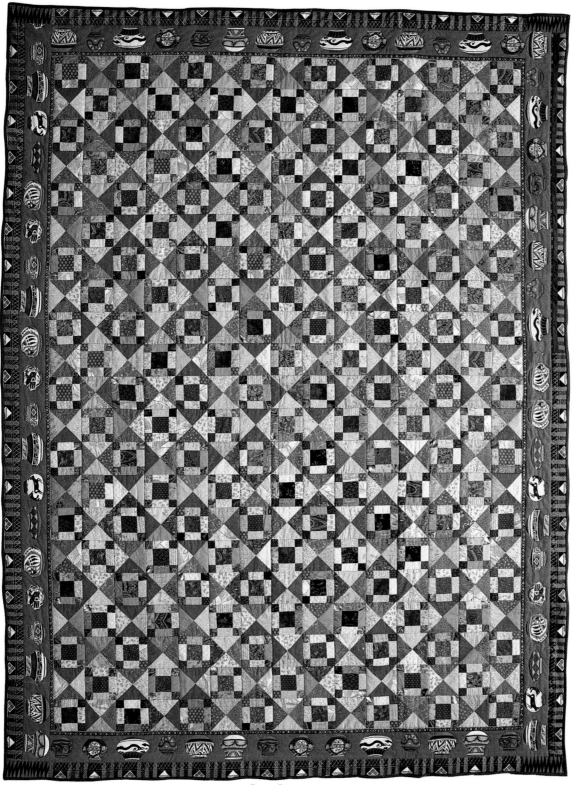

Four Corners

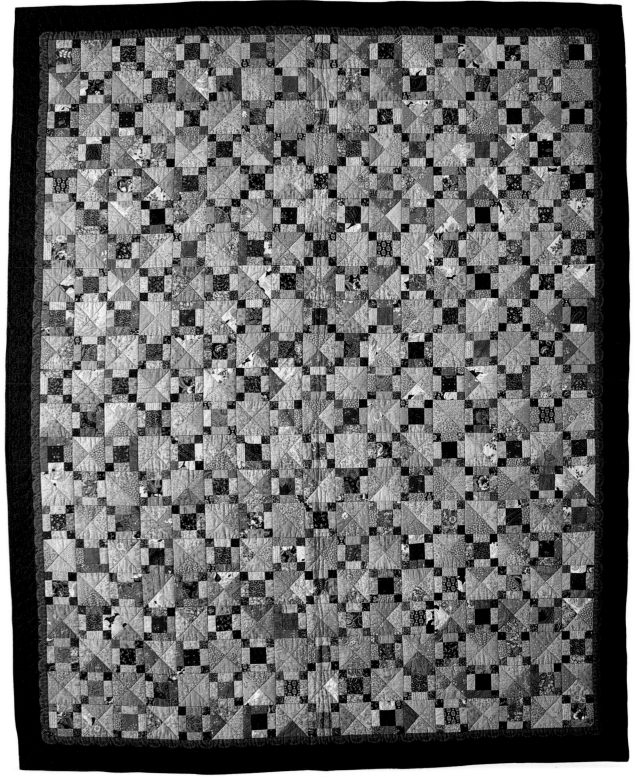

Sorbet

UNEVEN NINE PATCH
4" finished block

The Uneven Nine Patch is a scrap quilt of unusual simplicity. This two-block design uses an Uneven Nine Patch alternating with four triangles to form the pattern. The Uneven Nine Patches are sewn with the same method as a regular Nine Patch, the difference is the width of the strips. This "scrap-happy" quilt is made from assorted dark value fabrics with lighter fabrics as the background. A wonderful variation is to use equal amounts of medium-valued fabric and light-valued fabric for the 5¼" background fabrics.

WALL 36" x 44" WITHOUT BORDERS

9 blocks across by 11 blocks down
50 Uneven Nine Patch blocks
49 Triangle blocks

TWIN 60" x 84" WITHOUT BORDERS

15 blocks across by 21 blocks down
158 Uneven Nine Patch blocks
157 Triangle blocks

FULL/QUEEN 68" x 84" WITHOUT BORDERS

17 blocks across by 21 blocks down
179 Uneven Nine Patch blocks
178 Triangle blocks

KING 84" x 92" WITHOUT BORDERS

21 blocks across by 23 blocks down
242 Uneven Nine Patch blocks
241 Triangle blocks

FABRIC	WALL	TWIN	FULL/QUEEN	KING
2½" dark strips	4	10	12	16
2½" light strips	4	12	13	18
1½" dark strips	8	24	26	36
1½" light strips	8	20	24	32
5¼" light strips	7	20	23	31

OR

	WALL	TWIN	FULL/QUEEN	KING
an assortment of fabrics in dark values to equal	¾ yard	1⅞ yards	2⅛ yards	2¾ yards
and an assortment of fabrics in light values to equal	1¾ yards	4¾ yards	5⅜ yards	7¼ yards

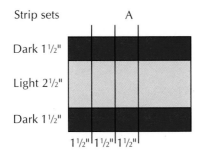

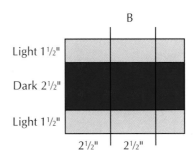

	WALL	TWIN	FULL/QUEEN	KING
Strip Set A	4	12	13	18
Cut sections A	100	316	358	484
Strip Set B	4	10	12	16
Cut sections B	50	158	179	242
Triangles	196	628	712	964

The strip sets needed for the Uneven Nine Patch are comprised of the wider 2½" strips in the center and the 1½" strips on either side. Strip Set A contains two 1½" dark strips and one 2½" light strip. Strip Set B contains two 1½" light strips and one 2½" dark strip. When cut into sections, Strip Set A is the outside columns of the Uneven Nine Patch and are cut at 1½" increments. Strip Set B is the center column and is cut at 2½" increments.

The second block needed to complete this quilt contains four triangles sewn together to form a 4½" unfinished square. The wider (5¼") strips are cut into 5¼" squares which are then cut twice diagonally into triangles.

INSTRUCTIONS

Refer to the basic instructions starting on page 5, if needed.

Step 1. Cut the number of strips needed from each fabric for the quilt size desired.

Step 2. Stack the strips needed for each strip set. Sew the required number of strip sets. Note that the 2½" strips are always in the center of the sets and the 1½" strips are on either side. Since this is a scrap quilt, mix up the fabrics within each strip set. For example, use two different darker fabrics in each Strip Set A, and two different lighter fabrics in Strip Set B.

Step 3. Press the seam allowances toward the dark strips in each set.

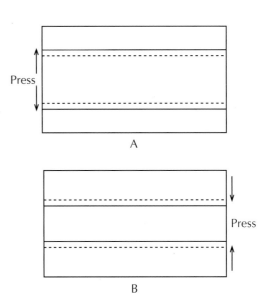

Step 4. Stack the strip sets, face down, in staggered piles. Cut Strip Set A into 1½" sections. Cut Strip Set B into 2½" sections.

Step 5. Review page 77 on chain piecing Nine Patches. Join the sections together to make the Uneven Nine Patches. Mix up the sections as you go to achieve the scrappy look.

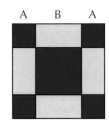

Step 6. Press the seam allowances toward the outside columns. These last seams are considered vertical seams. When assembling the quilt top, it is very helpful to keep these seams consistently vertical, or up and down, in the quilt top.

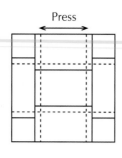

Step 7. Cut the 5¼" strips into 5¼" squares. Before lifting the squares from the cutting mat, cut them twice diagonally into triangles.

Step 8. To sew the triangle blocks, randomly pick up two triangles (again, you'll want to mix it up), and then lay them right sides together and stitch along a short edge. Chain piece all the triangles as shown. For variation, use medium and light fabrics in the background, always placing the medium triangle on the bottom when sewing the two triangles together.

Step 9. Working from the right side of the fabric, press the seam allowances toward the left.

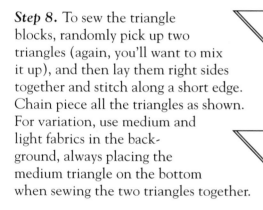

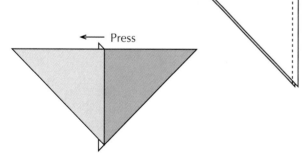

Press

Step 10. Stitch pairs of these double triangle units together along the long edge. Match up the seam lines, but note that the seam allowances are pressed in opposing directions to nest together. In the variation, the medium and light fabrics will alternate within each block.

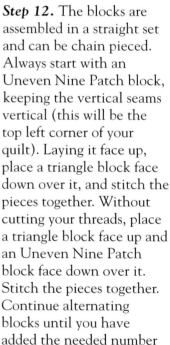

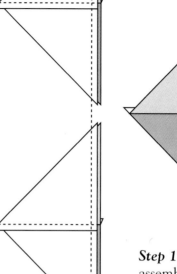

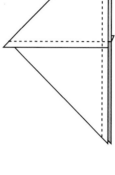

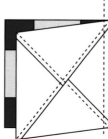

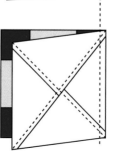

Step 11. Press these final seams in one direction. If desired, the "ears" at the corners of the blocks can be trimmed off.

Trim off ears

Step 12. The blocks are assembled in a straight set and can be chain pieced. Always start with an Uneven Nine Patch block, keeping the vertical seams vertical (this will be the top left corner of your quilt). Laying it face up, place a triangle block face down over it, and stitch the pieces together. Without cutting your threads, place a triangle block face up and an Uneven Nine Patch block face down over it. Stitch the pieces together. Continue alternating blocks until you have added the needed number of blocks.

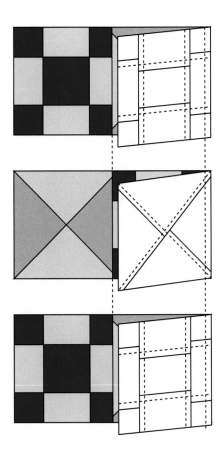

Step 13. Working again with the first set, add an Uneven Nine Patch to the first row. Add a triangle block to the second row, then continue alternating blocks to reach the bottom. Add the vertical rows in this manner until you have added the needed number of blocks across. Notice that the blocks in the four corners are Uneven Nine Patches.

Step 14. Press these seams toward the triangle blocks. The rows can now be sewn together, matching up the seam lines. Turn the seam lines joining the blocks in alternating directions across the rows. Press the final seams in either direction.

Step 15. Refer to the instructions starting on page 10 for adding borders, if desired.

DOUBLE IRISH CHAIN

Chocolate Lanes

DOUBLE IRISH CHAIN
70" x 90" without borders
10" finished block
32 X Blocks
31 Plain Blocks

Fabric requirements: Three fabrics of which Fabric 1 is the lightest (background).
Fabric 2 is the darkest and Fabric 3 is the connecting chain.

FABRIC #	YARDAGE	2½" STRIPS	6½"* STRIPS
1	3⅜ yards	20	10
2	2⅜ yards	32	
3	1⅜ yards	18	

Scrap Irish Chain: For best results, use lighter values for Fabric 1, medium values for Fabric 2, and darker values for Fabric 3. Cut the number of strips needed for each of the color values from various fabrics. When making the strip sets, mix it up! For example, try using three different medium value strips for Fabric 2 in Strip Set B.

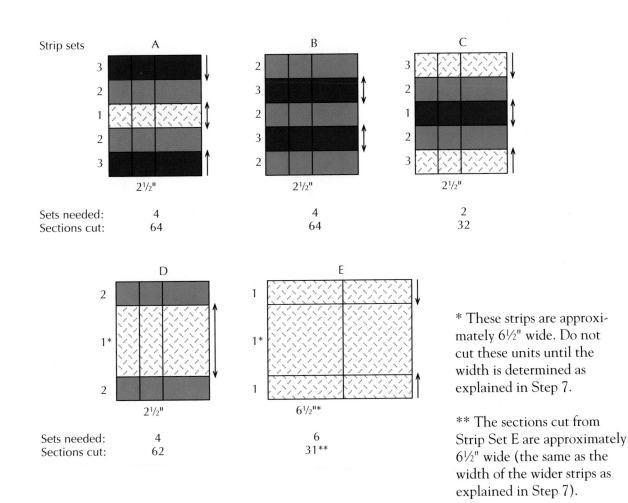

* These strips are approximately 6½" wide. Do not cut these units until the width is determined as explained in Step 7.

** The sections cut from Strip Set E are approximately 6½" wide (the same as the width of the wider strips as explained in Step 7).

INSTRUCTIONS

Refer to the basic instructions starting on page 5, if needed.

Step 1. Cut the required number of 2½" strips from each fabric. Do not cut the wider (6½"*) strips at this time. Make 32 X Blocks.

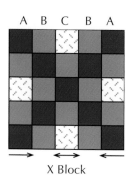

A B C B A

X Block

Step 2. Sew the Strip Sets A, B, and C, using a scant ¼" seam allowance.

Step 3. Press the seams in alternating directions toward the even-numbered fabrics in each strip set. The seam allowances are pressed so they will nest together at each seam line.

Step 4. Cut the required number of 2½" sections from each strip set.

Step 5. Chain piece the sections to make 32 X blocks. Begin with a Section A laying face up, then lay a Section B face down over Section A. Stitch the pieces together. Leave the thread intact and place the next Sections A and B in the machine, then stitch the pieces together. Sew together a total of 32 Sections A and B. Start back at the first block and open the sections. Lay a Section C face down over Section B and stitch the pieces together. Continue adding Sections C in this manner. After all the Sections C are joined, add Sections B, and then add Sections A to complete the blocks. Press the seams toward the Sections B in each block. Consider these last seams the vertical seams.

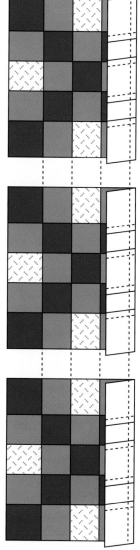

Step 6. Make 31 Plain Blocks.

Step 7. Strip Sets D and E each contain a wide strip of Fabric 1 in the center. To determine the width of the wider strips needed in Strip Sets D and E, you need to measure the width of the three center squares in the X Blocks. Measure from seam line to seam line, as shown, across the center of the block (not along the edge), and add ½" seam allowance to this measurement. This width should be approximately 6½", and the sections cut from Strip Set E will be cut this same width. Use this measurement to cut the number of wider strips needed of Fabric 1.

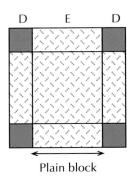

Plain block

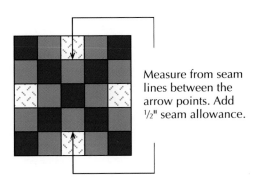

Measure from seam lines between the arrow points. Add ½" seam allowance.

Step 8. Strip Set D has a 2½" strip of Fabric 2 on either side of Fabric 1. Strip Set E has a 2½" strip of Fabric 1 on both sides of the wider strip of Fabric 1. To join the strips for Strip Set D, begin with a 2½" strip of Fabric 2 laying face up, then place the wide strip of Fabric 1 face down over it. Sew the strips together using a scant ¼" seam allowance. Chain piece the needed number of strip sets. Start back at the first set and turn the strips so the wide strip of fabric is laying face up, and add a 2½" strip of Fabric 2. Stitch the pieces together. Add the remaining strips of Fabric 2. Stitch Strip Set E in the same manner as Strip Set D, but replace a 2½" strip of Fabric 1 for the Fabric 2 strips.

Step 9. Press the seam allowances of Strip Set D toward the 2½" strips. Press the seam allowances of Strip Set E toward the wide strips of Fabric 1.

Step 10. Cut the strip sets into sections. Strip Set D is cut at 2½" increments. Strips Set E is cut at the same width as the wider strips cut in Step 7.

Step 11. Sew a Section D onto both sides of Section E, aligning the seam lines, as shown, to complete 31 Plain Blocks. Press the seams toward the Sections D. Consider the last seams the vertical seams.

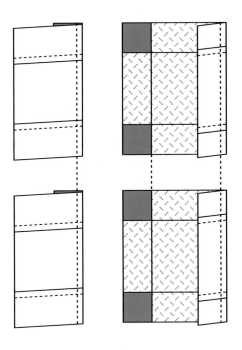

Step 12. The alternating blocks are now chain pieced together in a straight setting. When joining the blocks, keep the vertical seams in the same direction (up and down) throughout the quilt top. Begin with an X Block, face up, and lay a Plain Block face down on top of it. Matching the seam lines, stitch the pieces together using a scant ¼" seam allowance. Stitch off the end of the blocks, and leave the threads uncut. Next, lay a Plain Block face up and place an X Block face down on top of it and stitch together. Continue working in this manner until you have nine rows of two blocks. Start back at the first row and add an X Block to the Plain Block. Continue in this manner until you have completed nine rows of seven blocks.

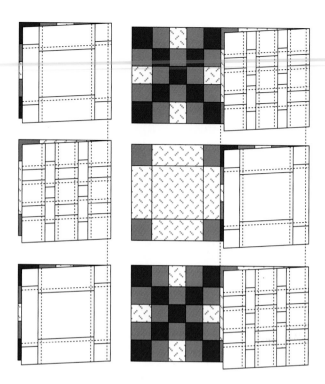

Step 13. This is a good time to lay out the quilt top just to make sure you have all the blocks in the correct order. Sew the rows together, matching up the seam lines. Turn the seam lines joining the blocks in alternating directions across the row. Press the final seams in either direction.

Step 14. Refer to the instructions starting on page 10 for adding borders, if desired.

BABY
DOUBLE IRISH CHAIN

◆

Sunflower Delight; graciously loaned to us by Kaye Johnson of Yorba Linda, California

BABY DOUBLE IRISH CHAIN
37½" x 52½" without borders
7½" finished square
18 X Blocks
17 Plain Blocks

This Irish Chain quilt reverses the color value of the fabrics, using the darkest as the background (Fabric 1) and the lightest as the center connecting fabric (Fabric 3).

FABRIC #	YARDAGE	2" STRIPS	5"* STRIPS
1	⅝ yard	9	
2	1 yard	16	
3	1⅜ yards	10	5

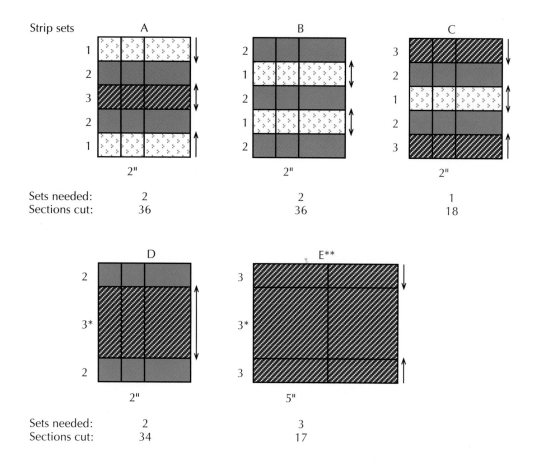

Strip sets

A — Sets needed: 2, Sections cut: 36
B — Sets needed: 2, Sections cut: 36
C — Sets needed: 1, Sections cut: 18
D — Sets needed: 2, Sections cut: 34
E** — Sets needed: 3, Sections cut: 17

*5" is the approximate width of these strips. Do not cut these until the width is figured as explained in Step 3.
**The sections cut from Strip Set E are cut at approximately 5" (the same as the width of the wider strips as explained in Step 3).

INSTRUCTIONS:

Refer to the basic instructions starting on page 5, if needed.

Step 1. Cut the number of 2" strips needed from each fabric. Do not cut the wider strips yet.

Step 2. Make 18 of X Block. Follow the instructions in the large Double Irish Chain quilt (page 98) for completing the 18 X Blocks, but cut the sections at 2" increments.

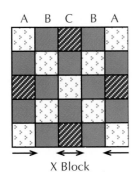

X Block

Step 3. Make 17 Plain Blocks. Strip Sets D and E each contain a wider strip of Fabric 3 in the center. To determine the width of the wider strips needed in Strip Sets D and E, you need to measure the width of the three center squares in the X blocks. Measure from seam line to seam line, as shown, across the center of the block (not along the edge). Add ½" seam allowance to this measurement. This width should be approximately 5" and the sections cut from Strip Set E will be cut this same width. Use this measurement to cut the number of wider strips needed of Fabric 3.

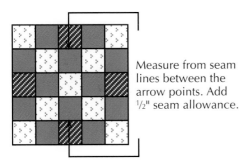

Measure from seam lines between the arrow points. Add ½" seam allowance.

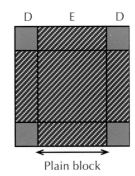

Plain block

Step 4. Follow the instructions in the large Double Irish Chain quilt (page 99) for completing the 17 Plain Blocks. Take care when cutting the sections from Strip Set E, and use the same width as the wider strip (as explained). Remember, the sections from Strip Set D are cut at 2" increments.

TRIPLE IRISH CHAIN

Irish Spice

TRIPLE IRISH CHAIN
73½" x 94½" without borders
10½" finished block
32 X Blocks
31 Plain Blocks

Fabric requirements: Four fabrics of which Fabric 1 is the background (lightest value),
Fabric 2 is the outer chain (medium value), Fabric 3 is the inner chain (medium dark value),
and Fabric 4 is the connecting chain (darkest value).

Scrap Irish Chain: Cut the number of strips needed for each of the color values from the various fabrics. When making the strip sets, mix it up! For example, try using four different medium-dark value strips for Fabric 3 in Strip Set B.

FABRIC #	YARDAGE	2" STRIPS	5" STRIPS*	8" STRIPS*
1	3 yards	7	6	7
2	2 yards	32		
3	2⅜ yards	39		
4	1⅜ yards	22		

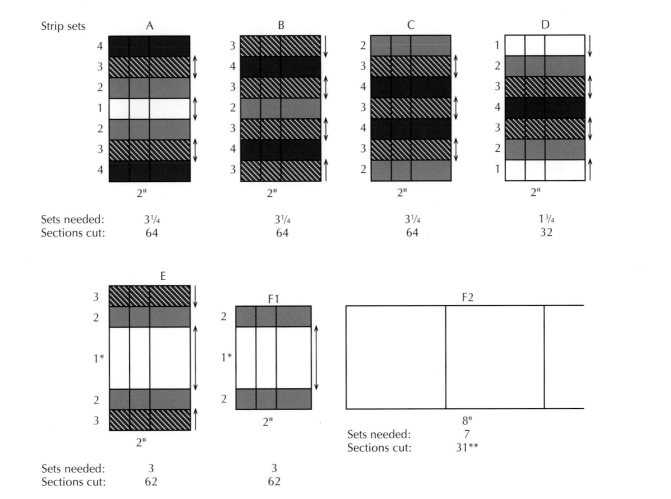

Strip sets	A	B	C	D
Sets needed:	3¼	3¼	3¼	1¾
Sections cut:	64	64	64	32

	E	F1	F2
Sets needed:	3	3	7
Sections cut:	62	62	31**

*These widths are approximate; the actual width of these strips is figured in Step 7.
**These sections are cut at increments the same width as the widest strips;
the actual width of these strips is figured in Step 7.

INSTRUCTIONS

Refer to the basic instructions starting on page 5, if needed.

Step 1. For Fabric 1, cut seven 2" strips. From these strips, cut 10½" off of two of the strips (one will be used in the quarter strip sets, and the balance of the strips will be used in the three-quarter strip sets). For Fabric 2, cut thirty-two 2" strips. From these strips, cut 10½" off of two of the strips (one will be used in the quarter strip sets, and the balance of the strips will be used in the three-quarter strip sets). Cut one strip into fourths (three will be used in the quarter strip sets). For Fabric 3, cut thirty-nine 2" strips. From these strips cut 10½" off of two strips (one will be used in the quarter strip sets, and the balance of the strips will be used in the three-quarter strip sets). Cut two strips into fourths for use in the quarter strip sets. For Fabric 4, cut twenty-two 2" strips. From these strips, cut 10½" off of two of the strips (one will be used in the quarter strip sets, and one strip will be used from the balance of the strips sets in the three-quarter strip sets). Cut one strip into fourths for use in the quarter strip sets.

X BLOCKS

Step 2. Sew the strips together for Strip Sets A, B, C, and D. The strips used in these strip sets are all 2" wide. Sew the required number of strip sets.

Step 3. Press the seam allowances toward the even-numbered fabric in each strip set.

Step 4. Cut the strip sets into 2" sections.

A B C D C B A

X Block

Step 5. Chain piece the sections to make 32 X blocks. Begin with Section A, face up, and lay Section B face down on Section A. Stitch the strips together. Without cutting the threads, stitch the next Sections A and B together. Continue in this manner to join together 32 of Sections A and B. Leave the threads intact and start back with the first block. Open the Sections A/B and place a Section C face down on B and stitch together. Add the Sections C to all the blocks. The D section is added to the blocks next and is the center section of the block. To complete the blocks, add Sections C, B, and A, in this order, to each block.

Step 6. Press the seams in alternating directions toward Sections C and A. Consider these last seams the vertical seams.

PLAIN BLOCKS

Step 7. Strip Set E consists of two 2" strips of Fabric 3, two 2" strips of Fabric 2, and one medium width strip of Fabric 1, in the following order: 3-2-1-2-3. Strip Set F1 consists of two 2" strips of Fabric 2 and one medium width strip of Fabric 1, in the following order: 2-1-2. To determine the width of the medium wide strips, you need to measure the width of the three center squares in Block X (the size is approximately 5"). Measure from seam line to seam line, as shown, across the center of the block (not along the edge). Add ½" seam allowance to this measurement. Cut six strips of this same width of Fabric 1. To determine the width of the widest strips (Strip Set F2), measure the five center squares in the X Block (the size is approximately 8"). Cut seven strips of this determined width of Fabric 1. From these strips (Strip Set F2), cut 31 squares of this same width.

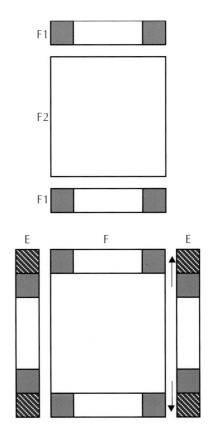

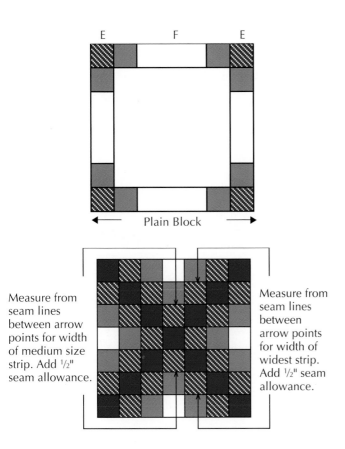

E   F   E

Plain Block

Measure from seam lines between arrow points for width of medium size strip. Add ½" seam allowance.

Measure from seam lines between arrow points for width of widest strip. Add ½" seam allowance.

Step 13. Refer to the instructions starting on page 10 for adding borders, if desired.

Step 8. Sew the required number of each Strip Set E and F1.

Step 9. Press the seam allowances in both Strip Sets E and F1 toward Fabric 2.

Step 10. Cut the strip sets into 2" sections.

Step 11. Sew Section F1 to the top and bottom of the squares that were cut from Strips F2 to form Section F. Press these seams toward F1. Then sew Section E to both sides of this section to complete the Plain Blocks. Press the seams toward Section E. Consider these last seams vertical seams. Make 31 Plain Blocks.

Step 12. The blocks are joined together in a straight setting. Follow the instructions on pages 99–100 of the Double Irish Chain quilt to complete the quilt top.

CHAPTER 6

TRIP AROUND THE WORLD

Hint of Mint

TRIP AROUND THE WORLD
85½" x 99½" including borders
2½" finished square

Fabric requirements: Six fabrics ranging in value from Fabric 1, the lightest, to Fabric 6, the darkest.

FABRIC #	YARDAGE	3" STRIPS
1	1¼ yards	13
2	1⅜ yards	15
3	1½ yards	16
4	1⅝ yards	18
5	1¾ yards	19
6	2 yards	21

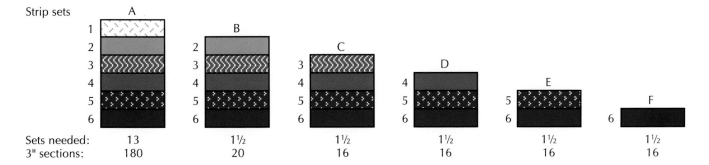

	A	B	C	D	E	F
Sets needed:	13	1½	1½	1½	1½	1½
3" sections:	180	20	16	16	16	16

INSTRUCTIONS

Refer to the basic instructions starting on page 5, if needed.

Step 1. Cut the required number of 3" strips from each fabric.

Step 2. Stack the strips needed for each strip set. When a half strip set is required, simply cut the full strips in half. Strip Set F isn't really a strip set, since it is a single strip and needs only to be cut into sixteen 3" squares.

Step 3. Sew the required number of strip sets. Press the seam allowances toward the even-numbered fabrics in each set.

Step 4. Stack and cut the strip sets into 3" sections.

Step 5. You now need to sew groups of sections together end-to-end into rows. These groups of sections, or rows, will be joined together to form two diagonal corners of the quilt top. Always keep Fabric 6 at the bottom of the sections. Make two sets of Group I, which are the center rows of each diagonal corner. Make four of each row of Groups II, III, IV, and V. Note that the rows in Group II contain three of Section A and one of Sections B, C, D, E, or F except for the last row, which contains only three of Section A. Each row in Group III contains two of Section A and one of Sections B, C, D, E, or F except for the last row, which has only two of Section A. Each row in Group IV has only one of Section A and one of Sections B, C, D, E, or F except for the last row, which is one of Section A. Each row in Group V has only one of Sections B, C, D, E, or F. Press these last seams toward Fabric 6 in each row.

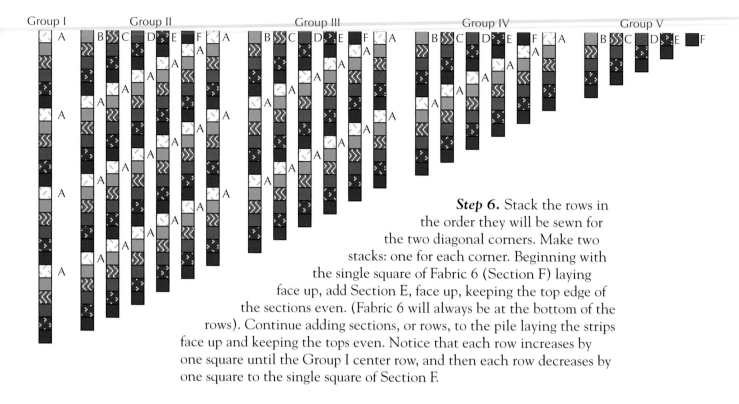

Group I   Group II   Group III   Group IV   Group V

Step 6. Stack the rows in the order they will be sewn for the two diagonal corners. Make two stacks: one for each corner. Beginning with the single square of Fabric 6 (Section F) laying face up, add Section E, face up, keeping the top edge of the sections even. (Fabric 6 will always be at the bottom of the rows). Continue adding sections, or rows, to the pile laying the strips face up and keeping the tops even. Notice that each row increases by one square until the Group I center row, and then each row decreases by one square to the single square of Section F.

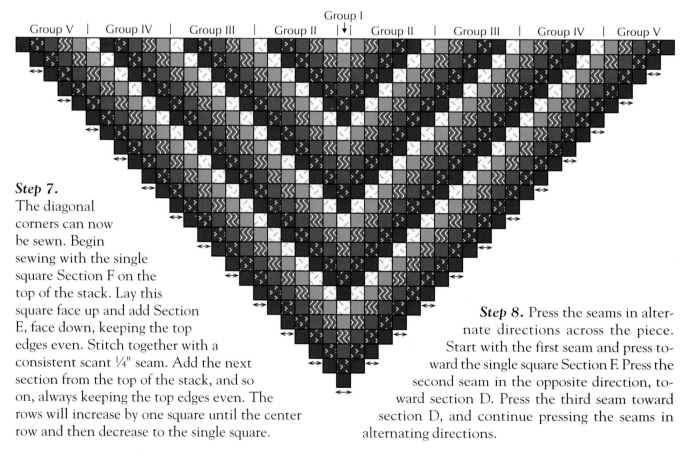

Group V | Group IV | Group III | Group II | Group I | Group II | Group III | Group IV | Group V

Step 7.
The diagonal corners can now be sewn. Begin sewing with the single square Section F on the top of the stack. Lay this square face up and add Section E, face down, keeping the top edges even. Stitch together with a consistent scant ¼" seam. Add the next section from the top of the stack, and so on, always keeping the top edges even. The rows will increase by one square until the center row and then decrease to the single square.

Step 8. Press the seams in alternate directions across the piece. Start with the first seam and press toward the single square Section F. Press the second seam in the opposite direction, toward section D. Press the third seam toward section D, and continue pressing the seams in alternating directions.

Step 9. Add four single rows between the two diagonal halves to lengthen the quilt. The single rows each consist of seven of Section A and one of Section B, as shown. Sew three of Section A together from top to bottom, keeping Fabric 6 at the bottom. Add a Section B to the top of the three Sections A. Sew four of Section A together from top to bottom, keeping Fabric 6 at the bottom.

Now sew the top of both of these rows together. The top of the four of Section A will be sewn to the top of Section B. Press the seams toward the even-numbered fabrics.

Step 10. Join these rows together, as shown, offsetting each row by one square. The diagonal corners can now be sewn to each side of the single rows. Press these last seams flat in one direction.

Single row

BABY
TRIP AROUND THE WORLD

Lilac Lace

BABY TRIP AROUND THE WORLD
50½" x 56" including borders
2" finished square

Six fabrics ranging in value from Fabric 1, the lightest, to Fabric 6, the darkest.

FABRIC #	YARDAGE	2½" STRIPS
1	½ yard	6
2	⅝ yard	7
3	⅝ yard	8
4	¾ yard	9
5	⅞ yard	10
6	⅞ yard	11

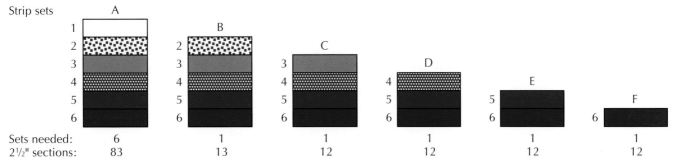

Strip sets

	A	B	C	D	E	F
Sets needed:	6	1	1	1	1	1
2½" sections:	83	13	12	12	12	12

INSTRUCTIONS

Refer to the basic instructions starting on page 5, if needed.

Step 1. Cut the required number of 2½" strips from each fabric.

Step 2. Stack the strips needed for each strip set. Strip Set F isn't really a strip set, since it is a single strip and needs only to be cut into twelve 2½" squares.

Step 3. Sew the required number of strip sets together. Press the seam allowances toward the even-numbered fabrics in each set.

Step 4. Stack and cut the strip sets into 2½" sections.

Step 5. You now need to sew groups of sections together end-to-end into rows. These groups of sections will be joined together to form two diagonal corners of the quilt top. Always keep Fabric 6 at the bottom of the sections. Make two sets of Group I, which are the center rows of each diagonal corner. Make four rows each of Groups II, III, and IV. Note that the rows in Group II contain two of Section A and one of Sections B, C, D, E, or F except for the last row, which contains only two of Section A. Each row in Group III contains one of Section A and one each of Sections B, C, D, E, or F except for the last row, which has only one of Section A. Each row in Group IV is only one each of Sections B, C, D, E, or F. Press these last seams toward Fabric 6 in each row.

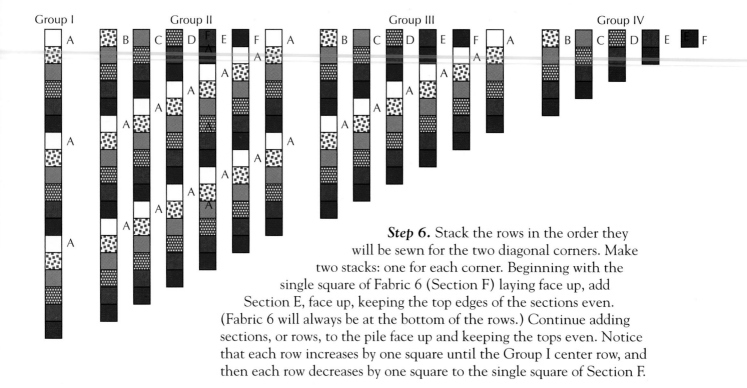

Step 6. Stack the rows in the order they will be sewn for the two diagonal corners. Make two stacks: one for each corner. Beginning with the single square of Fabric 6 (Section F) laying face up, add Section E, face up, keeping the top edges of the sections even. (Fabric 6 will always be at the bottom of the rows.) Continue adding sections, or rows, to the pile face up and keeping the tops even. Notice that each row increases by one square until the Group I center row, and then each row decreases by one square to the single square of Section F.

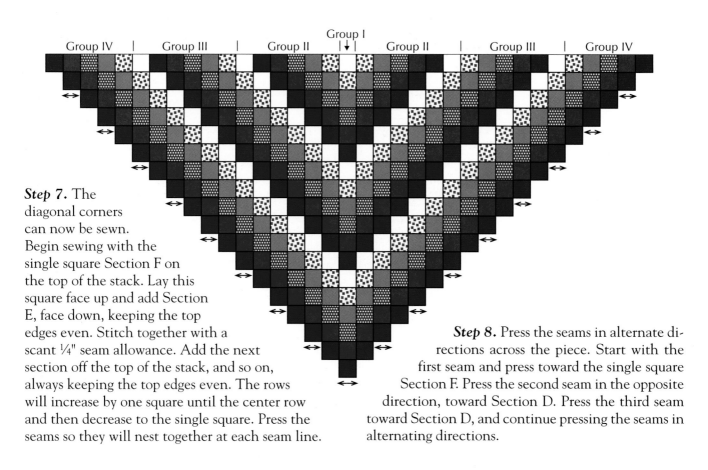

Step 7. The diagonal corners can now be sewn. Begin sewing with the single square Section F on the top of the stack. Lay this square face up and add Section E, face down, keeping the top edges even. Stitch together with a scant ¼" seam allowance. Add the next section off the top of the stack, and so on, always keeping the top edges even. The rows will increase by one square until the center row and then decrease to the single square. Press the seams so they will nest together at each seam line.

Step 8. Press the seams in alternate directions across the piece. Start with the first seam and press toward the single square Section F. Press the second seam in the opposite direction, toward Section D. Press the third seam toward Section D, and continue pressing the seams in alternating directions.

Step 9. Add one single row between the two diagonal halves to lengthen the quilt. The single row consists of five of Section A and one of Section B, as shown. Sew two of Section A together from top to bottom, keeping Fabric 6 at the bottom. Add a Section B to the top of the two Sections A. Sew three of Section A together, from top to bottom, keeping Fabric 6 at the bottom. Now sew the top of both of these rows together. The top of the three Sections A will be sewn to the top of Section B. Press the seams toward the even-numbered fabrics.

Step 10. Sew the diagonal corners to each side of the single row. Press these last seams flat in one direction.

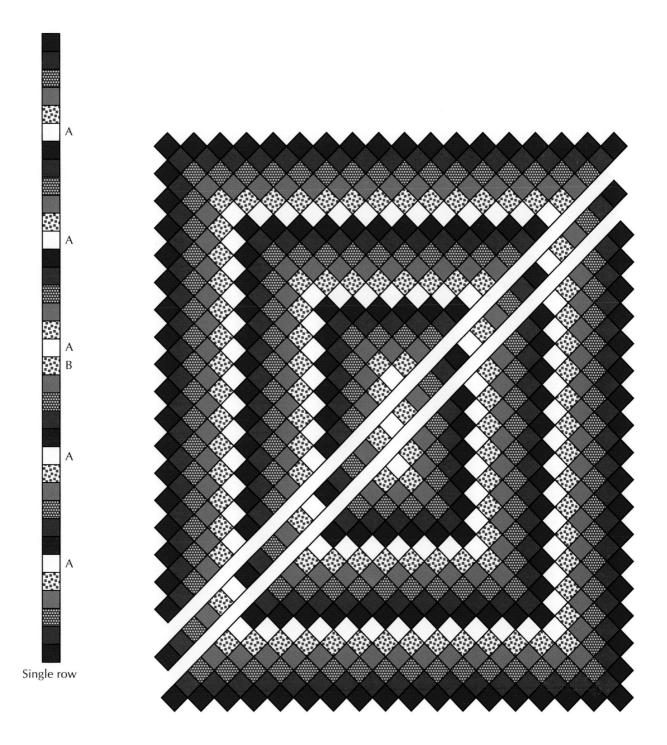

Single row

COLORS AROUND THE WORLD

Colors Around the World

COLORS AROUND THE WORLD
85½" x 103½" including borders
2½" finished square

Fabric requirements: This variation of Trip Around the World employs six fabrics each of four different color families. Rather than repeating the same fabric sequence throughout the quilt, different fabrics and colors are used in each sequence.
To differentiate between each fabric group, we have used the colors in the quilt shown. Fabric 1 in each group is the lightest value, and Fabric 6 is the darkest value in each group.

GREEN FABRIC #	YARDAGE	BURGUNDY FABRIC#	YARDAGE
1	⅛ yard	1	⅜ yard
2	⅛ yard	2	⅜ yard
3	¼ yard	3	⅜ yard
4	¼ yard	4	½ yard
5	¼ yard	5	½ yard
6	⅜ yard	6	½ yard

TURQUIOSE FABRIC #	YARDAGE	ORANGE FABRIC#	YARDAGE
1	½ yard	1	⅝ yard
2	½ yard	2	¾ yard
3	½ yard	3	¾ yard
4	⅝ yard	4	¾ yard
5	⅝ yard	5	¾ yard
6	⅝ yard	6	¾ yard

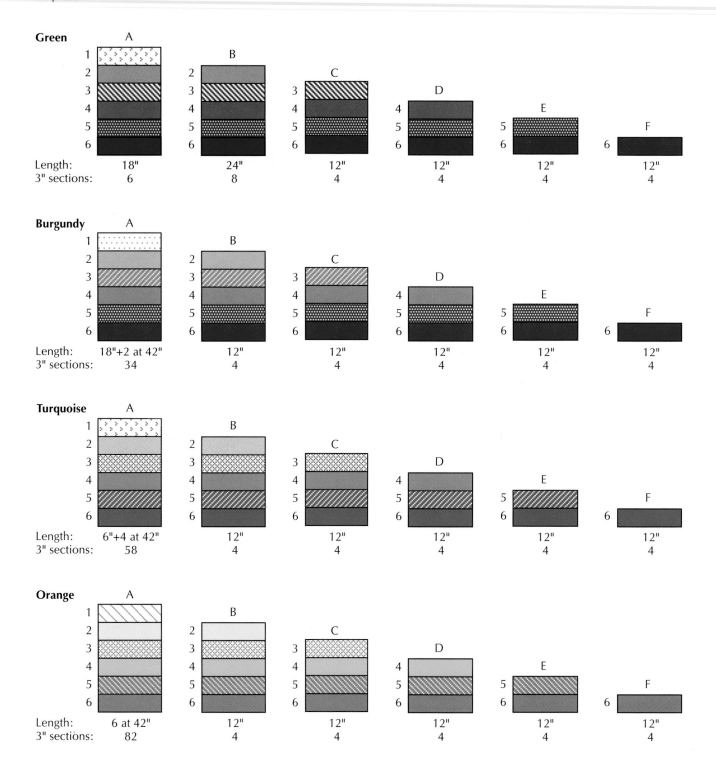

Green

	A	B	C	D	E	F
Length:	18"	24"	12"	12"	12"	12"
3" sections:	6	8	4	4	4	4

Burgundy

	A	B	C	D	E	F
Length:	18"+2 at 42"	12"	12"	12"	12"	12"
3" sections:	34	4	4	4	4	4

Turquoise

	A	B	C	D	E	F
Length:	6"+4 at 42"	12"	12"	12"	12"	12"
3" sections:	58	4	4	4	4	4

Orange

	A	B	C	D	E	F
Length:	6 at 42"	12"	12"	12"	12"	12"
3" sections:	82	4	4	4	4	4

INSTRUCTIONS

Refer to the basic instructions starting on page 5, if needed.

Step 1. Cut the required number of 3" strips from each fabric.

Step 2. Stack the strips needed for each strip set of each color group. Cut the strips to the needed length before sewing them into the strip set. You may want to allow an extra inch or so for squaring up the strips. Strip Set F isn't really a strip set, since it is a single strip and needs only to be cut into sixteen 3" squares.

Step 3. Sew the required number of strip sets. Press the seam allowances toward the even-numbered fabrics in each set.

Step 4. Stack and cut the strip sets into 3" sections.

Step 5. You now need to sew groups of sections together end-to-end into rows. These groups of sections, or rows, will be joined together to form two diagonal corners of the quilt top. Always keep Fabric 6 at the bottom of the sections, and the orange-colored sections at the bottom of the rows. Make two sets of Group I, which are the center rows of each diagonal corner. Each row consists of a Section A from each of the four color families. Note that the green section is at the top of the row, followed by the burgundy section, and then the turquoise and orange sections are at the bottom. Make four of each row in Groups II, III, IV, and V. Note that each row in Group II contains one Section A of orange, turquoise, and burgundy, and one each of Sections B, C, D, E, or F of the green except for the last row, which contains only three of Section A. Each row in Group III contains one of Section A in turquoise and orange, and one of Sections B, C, D, E, or F in burgundy except for the last row, which has only two of Section A. Each row in Group IV has only one orange Section A and one each of Sections B, C, D, E, or F in turquoise except for the last row, which has one of Section A. Each row in Group V is only one each of Sections B, C, D, E, or F of the orange. Press these last seams toward Fabric 6 in each row.

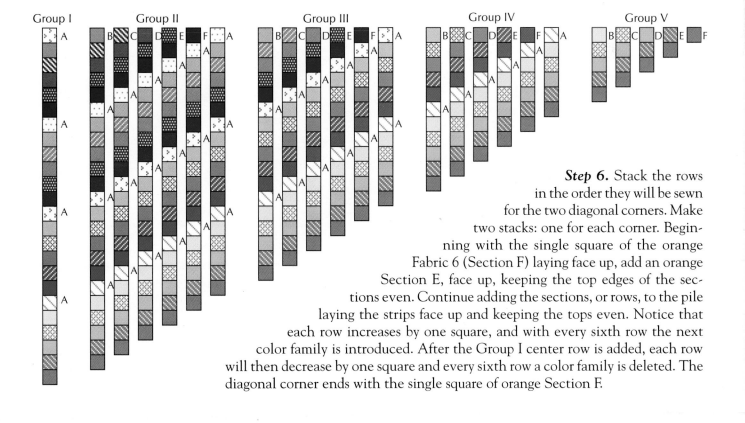

| Group I | Group II | Group III | Group IV | Group V |

Step 6. Stack the rows in the order they will be sewn for the two diagonal corners. Make two stacks: one for each corner. Beginning with the single square of the orange Fabric 6 (Section F) laying face up, add an orange Section E, face up, keeping the top edges of the sections even. Continue adding the sections, or rows, to the pile laying the strips face up and keeping the tops even. Notice that each row increases by one square, and with every sixth row the next color family is introduced. After the Group I center row is added, each row will then decrease by one square and every sixth row a color family is deleted. The diagonal corner ends with the single square of orange Section F.

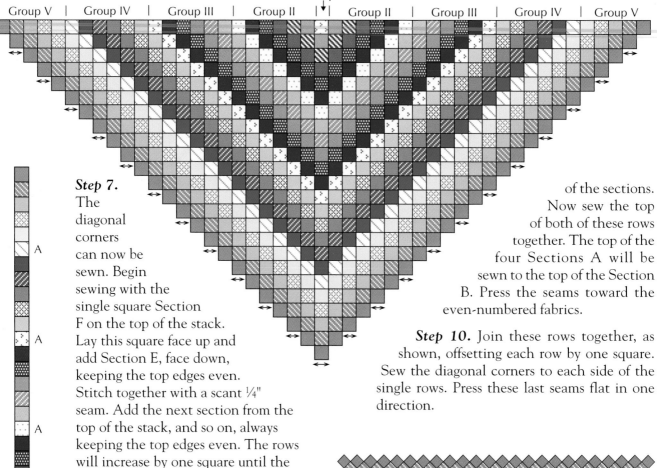

Step 7. The diagonal corners can now be sewn. Begin sewing with the single square Section F on the top of the stack. Lay this square face up and add Section E, face down, keeping the top edges even. Stitch together with a scant ¼" seam. Add the next section from the top of the stack, and so on, always keeping the top edges even. The rows will increase by one square until the center row and then decrease to the single square.

Step 8. Press the seams in alternate directions across the piece. Start with the first seam and press toward the single square Section F. Press the second seam in the opposite direction toward Section D. Press the third seam toward Section D, and continue pressing the seams alternating directions.

Step 9. Add four single rows between the two diagonal halves to lengthen the quilt. The single rows each consist of two orange Sections A, two turquoise Sections A, two burgundy Sections A, and one each of green Sections A and B, as shown. Sew the turquoise sections to the top of the orange sections. Sew the burgundy sections to the turquoise sections. Sew the green Section A to one of the turquoise sections and the green Section B to the top of the other turquoise section. Always keep Fabric 6 at the bottom

of the sections. Now sew the top of both of these rows together. The top of the four Sections A will be sewn to the top of the Section B. Press the seams toward the even-numbered fabrics.

Step 10. Join these rows together, as shown, offsetting each row by one square. Sew the diagonal corners to each side of the single rows. Press these last seams flat in one direction.

Single row

CHAPTER 7

JAMAICA

Jamaica

Not Quite Amish

JAMAICA
82" x 98" including borders
2" finished square

Seven fabrics ranging in value from Fabric 1, the lightest, to Fabric 7, the darkest.

FABRIC #	YARDAGE
1	1⅜ yard including border accent squares
2	1½ yards
3	1½ yards
4	1⅛ yards
5	⅞ yard
6	1 yard
7	2⅜ yards including border

Strip sets

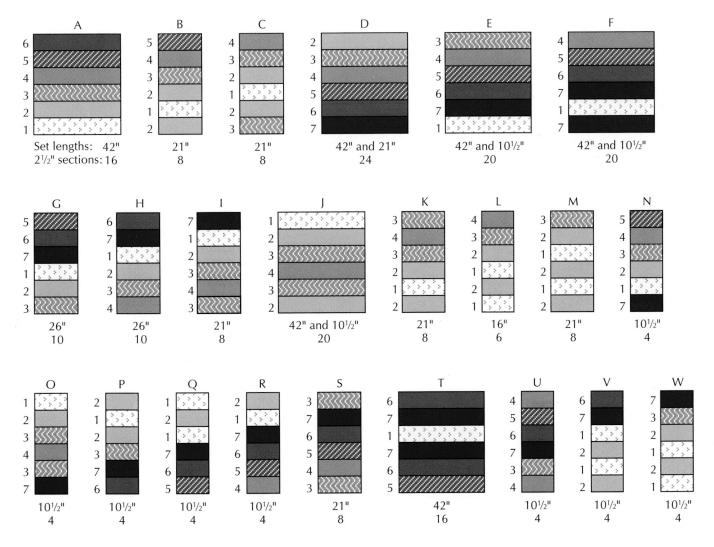

A	B	C	D	E	F
Set lengths: 42"	21"	21"	42" and 21"	42" and 10½"	42" and 10½"
2½" sections: 16	8	8	24	20	20

G	H	I	J	K	L	M	N
26"	26"	21"	42" and 10½"	21"	16"	21"	10½"
10	10	8	20	8	6	8	4

O	P	Q	R	S	T	U	V	W
10½"	10½"	10½"	10½"	21"	42"	10½"	10½"	10½"
4	4	4	4	8	16	4	4	4

Strip sets (continued)

	a	b	c	d	e	f	g
	5	6	7	1	2	3	4
	4	5	6	7	1	2	3
	3	4	5	6	7	1	2
	2	3	4	5	6	7	1
	1 9"	2 10½"	3 10½"	4 10½"	5 10½"	6 10½"	7 10½"
Set lengths:	16"	21"	21"	21"	21"	21"	21"
2¼" sections:	3	4	4	4	4	4	4
2¼" revised sections:	3	4	4	4	4	4	4

	h	i	j	k	l
	3	2	1	2	1
	4	3	2	1	2
	3	4	3	2	1
	2	3	4	3	2
	1 6"	2 6"	3 6"	4 6"	3 6"
Set lengths:	10½"	10½"	10½"	10½"	10½"
2¼" sections:	2	2	2	2	2
2¼" revised sections:	2	2	2	2	2

Unit I—Make two

A B C C̲ B A̲ D E F G H I J J̲ K L M M̲ L M̲ M L K J̲ J I H G F E D A̲ B C̲ C B A

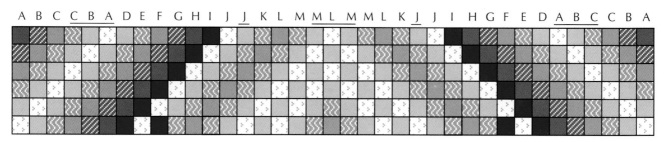

Unit II—Make two

D E F T̲ T F̲ E̲ D̲ A D̲ S R Q P O̲ J I H G H I J̲ O P Q R S D̲ A D E F T T̲ F E D

Unit III—Make two

J J̲ K W V G U S̲ D E F T̲ T F̲ E̲ D A N H̲ N A D̲ E̲ F̲ T T̲ F E D S̲ U G V W K J̲ J

*The underlined sections need to be turned upside down before sewing into the units.

◆ 124 ◆

l k j i h g f e d c b a g f e d c b a b c d e f g a b c d e f g h i j k l

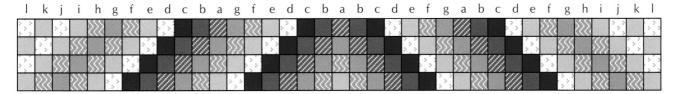

INSTRUCTIONS

Review the basic instructions starting on page 5, if needed.

Step 1. For Fabric 1, cut eighteen 2½" strips. From these strips, leave five strips full length. Cut five of the strips in half to yield ten 21" lengths. Cut two of the strips into two 26" and two into 16" lengths (one of each length from each strip). Cut four of the strips in fourths to yield sixteen 10½" lengths. Cut one strip into one 10½" length, one 9" length, and one 6" length. The remaining strip will be cut into sixteen 2½" squares for the accent in the border. (It is not necessary to cut these squares at this time.)

For Fabric 2, cut nineteen 2½" strips. From these strips, leave four full length. Cut seven of the strips in half to yield fourteen 21" lengths. Cut two of the strips into two 26" lengths and two into 16" lengths (one of each length from each strip). Cut five of the strips in fourths to yield twenty 10½" lengths. Cut one strip into one 16" and one 5" length.

For Fabric 3, cut nineteen 2½" strips. From these strips, leave five full length. Cut seven strips in half to yield fourteen 21" lengths. Cut two strips into two 26" lengths and two 16" lengths (one of each length from each strip). Cut four strips in fourths to yield sixteen 10½" lengths. Cut one strip into one 10½" length and two 6" lengths.

For Fabric 4, cut fifteen 2½" strips. From these strips, leave five full length. Cut five strips in half to yield nine 21" lengths. Cut one strip into one 26" length and one 16" length. Cut three strips in fourths to yield twelve 10½" lengths. Cut one strip into one 16" length and one 6" length.

For Fabric 5, cut eleven 2½" strips. From these strips, leave five full length. Cut three strips in half to yield six 21" lengths. Cut one strip into one 26" length and one 16" length. Cut two strips in fourths to yield seven 10½" lengths.

For Fabric 6, cut thirteen 2½" strips. From these strips leave six full length. Cut three of the strips in half to yield six 21" lengths. Cut two strips in fourths to yield eight 10½" lengths. Cut two strips into two 26" lengths.

For Fabric 7, cut fourteen 2½" strips. From these strips, leave six full length. Cut three strips in half to yield six 21" lengths. Cut two strips in fourths to yield eight 10½" lengths. Cut one strip into one 21" length and two 10½" lengths. Cut two strips into two 26" lengths and two 10½" lengths (one of each length from each strip).

Step 2. Cut the required number of 2½" strips from each fabric. Stack the strips in piles according to their fabric number and their length.

Step 3. Stack the strips needed for each strip set. Stack the strips laying face up, starting with the strip on the bottom and working up to the top. The strips will be in the order they will be sewn and can be picked up off the top of the pile and added to the strip set. It would be wise to mark each strip set with its corresponding letter (A, B, C, *etc.*). Use a sticky note on the top strip in the sets as explained in the Helpful Hints on page 16. You will have some strips remaining to use later in the Revised Unit IV.

Step 4. Sew the required number of strip sets together. Keep track of the top strip in each set, as this will be the top square in each section. To complete the center of the quilt design, a horizontal odd row needs to be added. This is achieved easily by revising some of the strip sets, or adding a partial strip to the bottom of some of the strip sets. The sections cut from these revised strips will be sewn together in what we call the Revised Unit IV. Use the remaining strips and add these strips to the strip sets as follows:

Sew the 9" strip of Fabric 1 to Strip Set a.
Sew the 10½" strip of Fabric 2 to Strip Set b.

Sew the 10½" strip of Fabric 3 to Strip Set c.
Sew the 10½" strip of Fabric 4 to Strip Set d.
Sew the 10½" strip of Fabric 5 to Strip Set e.
Sew the 10½" strip of Fabric 6 to Strip Set f.
Sew the 10½" strip of Fabric 7 to Strip Set g.
Sew the 6" strip of Fabric 1 to Strip Set h.
Sew the 6" strip of Fabric 2 to Strip Set i.
Sew the 6" strip of Fabric 3 to Strip Set j.
Sew the 6" strip of Fabric 4 to Strip Set k.
Sew the 6" strip of Fabric 3 to Strip Set l.

Step 5. When pressing the strip sets, press the seam allowances of the following strip sets toward the top strip in each set: A, C, D, F, J, K, M, N, O, Q, S, T, U, V, h, j, and l. Press the seam allowances of the following strip sets toward the bottom strips: B, E, G, L, P, R, W, i, and k. Press the seam allowances, first in one direction and then in the other direction, of the following strips sets: H, I, a, b, c, d, e, f, and g.

Step 6. Cut the strip sets into 2½" sections. Stack the cut sections from each strip set in one pile with the top of all the sections in the same direction. Line up the piles in alphabetical order, as this will help speed up the process of stacking the units.

Step 7. Stack the sections into piles in the order they will be used in each unit. Take care to reverse or turn upside down those sections that need to be turned. Stack the sections following the illustration on pages 124–125. You can stack the sections, face up, from the left or right since the units are the same from one side to the other. Stack two of Unit I, two of Unit II, two of Unit III, one of Unit IV, and one of Revised Unit IV.

Step 8. Sew the sections together into units. The seam allowances will nest together at every seam line. The strip sets that were pressed in both directions should be made to alternate with those seams that were pressed in one direction.

Step 9. Press the seam allowances of Units I and Units III to the right and Units II and IV to the left.

Step 10. It is helpful to lay the completed units on a floor, in the order they will be joined together. Notice that the units in the bottom half of the quilt are turned upside down, and are the mirror image of the top units. The pressed seam allowances will nest together. Sew the units together in the order shown. Press these last seams flat in one direction.

Step 11. For the borders, cut one 2½" strip of Fabric 1. Cut the strip into sixteen 2½" squares for the border accent squares (Z). Cut sixteen 2½" strips of Fabric 7. Trim off the selvages and seam the strips together end-to-end into one long strip. Press the seams open.

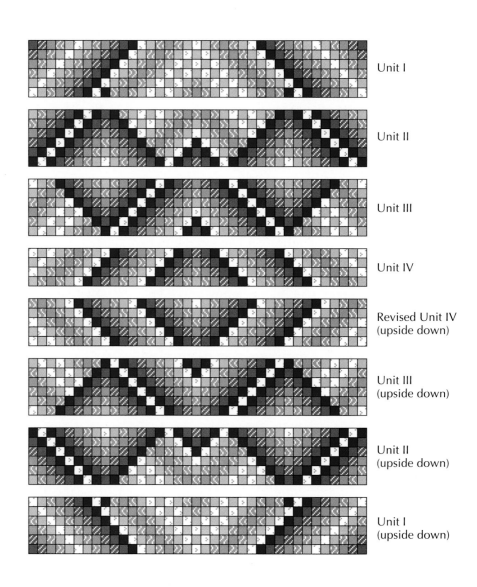

Unit I

Unit II

Unit III

Unit IV

Revised Unit IV
(upside down)

Unit III
(upside down)

Unit II
(upside down)

Unit I
(upside down)

Step 12. From the long strip, cut the following lengths: four 32½" lengths (A), two 14½" lengths (B), six 30½" lengths (C), two 18½" lengths (D), four 28½" lengths (E), four 26½" lengths (F), and two 34½" lengths (G). Because the sewn ¼" seam allowances vary from one person to another, measure your quilt for accurate lengths, and then adjust the lengths, if needed.

Step 13. For the side outer borders, sew together two sets of the following strips: E to Z to C to Z to E. Press the seams toward the Z squares. For the side inner borders, sew together two sets of the following strips: F to Z to G to Z to F. Press the seams toward the Z squares. Sew one of each set together, as shown. Press the seam toward the outer border. For the top and bottom outer borders, sew together two sets of the following strips: A to Z to B to Z to A. Press the seams toward the Z squares. For the top and bottom inner borders, sew together two sets of the following strips: C to Z to D to Z to C. Press the seams toward the Z squares. Sew one of each set together, as shown. Press the seam toward the outer border.

Step 14. Follow the instructions starting on page 10 to add the borders, if desired.

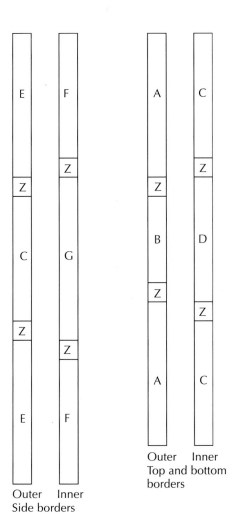

Outer   Inner
Side borders

Outer   Inner
Top and bottom borders

ABOUT THE AUTHORS

After viewing a quilt made by Blanche, many people have commented on the ability she has to put fabrics and colors together to produce such beautiful creations. Yet, Blanche has never had any formal education in color—she just enjoys the aspects of blending and mixing hues and patterns. Blanche's interest in color began at an early age from watching her father mix paint. Being the local wallpaper hanger and painter, he would stir, add pigment, and explain what the results would be. From her mother, Blanche learned how the careful arrangement of colors in the large flower garden would enhance each other. The purple iris was always behind the yellow tulips, the peonies with their large pink, red, and white blooms would be near the purple larkspurs or the early lavender phlox, and the orange and yellow marigolds always sported a border of purple ageratum and blue/purple lobelia—always the perfect compliment in colors. At age 13, Blanche made her first quilt—a *Sunbonnet Sue*—using fabrics from a scrap bag. Through the years, Blanche has made hundreds of quilts. Had she known then what she knows today, Blanche vows her children would not have been allowed to jump on their beds—on the quilts, of course!

As the youngest of Blanche's daughters, Dalene has always had sewing and fabrics as a part of her life. Dalene remembers sharing a bedroom with a sewing machine, and many nights being lulled to sleep by the hum of the machine as her mother worked. At age 13, Dalene received her first sewing machine (although at the time she secretly wished the box contained a stereo) and she made her first quilt—a *Lone Star*—when she was 16. Dalene admits to failing Home Economics, due to the fact that she insisted on doing things the way her mother taught her—not how the teacher wanted things done. Today, Dalene machine quilts over 125 quilts a year, in addition to teaching at quilt guilds and shops around the country.